PRIESTHOOD

Books by the same author:

Words of Comfort, ST PAUL Publications, 1990
Words of Encouragement, ST PAUL Publications, 1992

PRIESTHOOD
A Life Open to Christ

Compiled by
Daniel P. Cronin

ST PAULS

Cover picture: King of Kings and Great High Priest.

ST PAULS Publishing
187 Battersea Bridge Road, London SW11 3AS, UK
www.stpaulspublishing.com

Copyright © ST PAULS UK, 2009
ISBN 978-0-85439-762-4

Set by TuKan DTP, Stubbington, Fareham, UK
Printed by Melita Press, Malta

ST PAULS is an activity of the priests and brothers
of the Society of St Paul who proclaim the Gospel
through the media of social communication.

Contents

Foreword

I am very pleased to commend this book *Priesthood: A life open to Christ*. Its publication is very timely as we seek to respond to the invitation of Pope Benedict XVI to hold a "Year of the Priesthood".

The life of a priest is, generally speaking, a happy and satisfying one. The testimony in this book, from so many distinguished people, is evidence of how much inspiration is to be found in the call of Christ to men to share in the ordained priesthood.

Any young man – and not so young man – sensing a call from the Lord will find in the life of a priest great challenges as well as profound consolation.

I thank all who have been involved in the preparation and publication of this book, particularly Canon Daniel Cronin.

During this Year of the Priesthood we are invited to cherish our priests, to pray for vocations and to thank God for the great service of the priesthood in the Catholic Church today.

+ Vincent Nichols
Archbishop of Westminster

Preface

Pope Benedict XVI's announcement that he was designating a Year of the Priesthood to begin on 19 June 2009, coinciding with the 150th anniversary of the death of St John Vianney, Curé d'Ars and Patron Saint of Parish Priests, came, I think, as a very pleasant surprise to most priests. This special year for us is undoubtedly opportune and welcome. As Francis Cardinal George of Chicago alludes to at the beginning of his article, the priesthood has come through some difficult times of late because of the appalling misdemeanours of a few. It is, therefore, timely to turn the focus on the majority of priests who try to live to the best of their ability lives of integrity. I hope this book may be an inspiration and an encouragement for them to continue to persevere and thrive.

As priests, our lives are dedicated to the service of the people entrusted to our care; they frequently teach us far more than we ever impart to them and they are often much closer to God than we are. I have dedicated this book to one such woman, Celia McLennan. Before her death earlier this year at the age of 101, she said to me: "If, when I get to the pearly gates, God should turn his back on me and not allow me into heaven, then all the consolations and comforts of my faith will have been enough for me!" If we, Catholic priests, have any doubts about the usefulness of our ministry, I think such a faith-filled statement should dispel them. The mutual love and respect priests and people have for each other strikes me as being as unique and as strong as ever.

From the outset I was convinced that the hallmark of this book must be sheer authenticity. I wanted the contributors to communicate in that beautiful phrase to be found on the coat of arms of the Venerable John Henry

Newman: *Cor ad cor loquitur*, (*Heart speaks to heart*); so that the heart of every reader might be touched by real, lived experiences and not by dry theoretical treatises. I would like to thank profoundly every person who has contributed to this anthology; each one has responded with great generosity and enthusiasm.

The contributors have written from a depth of insight and with a diversity of content which reflect the varied nature of their work and ministry within the priesthood. It has been difficult to determine how best to present their work. Therefore the ordering of the articles has been done purely on an alphabetical by author basis, thereby making a compilation such as this something to be dipped into rather than read from cover to cover.

It is my hope that this book will echo to each reader the phrase written on the memorial card for Fr Gerry Fitzsimons, a missionary priest in South Africa, originally from Coleshill in Birmingham, who was murdered in 2004: "I thank Our Lord Jesus Christ, the source of all my strength, for showing confidence in me by appointing me his minister."

Daniel P. Cronin

My Touch on God Within My Darkness

Fr Cyril Axelrod

I was born deaf with good sight and I was very young in the 1950s. My kind-hearted Jewish father used to take me with him visiting different homes for the elderly and disabled people on Sundays. It always brought me wonder to witness their joy and faith even when they did not receive a visit from their families or friends.

It happened one day when my father decided to take me to visit a home for deafblind people. I had no idea what it meant to be deafblind or how to communicate with them. I slowly approached a gentle deafblind man sitting on the comfortable sofa but struggled with my shyness because I did not know how to communicate with him. He sensed my nearness and held out his right hand to me. My small hand touched his as the sign of beginning communication. He taught me the fingerspelling on my hands. It melted my fear and shyness of unknowing and it moved me closer to him. My father's face and heart beamed with a smile. It became the seed of my future mission even though I was totally unaware that I would eventually become fully blind later in life.

After over forty years I was diagnosed with progressive blindness. It shattered my hope and faith as a young Redemptorist priest (after I converted to Catholicism) but the seed of my father's love for disabled people had been planted in my heart. I began to sprout with a renewed faith in overcoming the fear of being unknown. That opened the way for me to affirm my faith and trust in God despite the endless obstacles and difficulties in my life of today and tomorrow.

The fear of being unknown can easily lead to losing faith or clinging to shyness. Jesus used the same phrase thirty-two times in the Gospel – "Do not be afraid". It is the matter of faith which strengthens one's confidence and trust to know what is unknown. For example, it is quite natural to feel overwhelmed when not being able to understand what deafblindness means or not knowing how to communicate with the deafblind person. To approach him or her and ask him or her to teach you the way of communication, will melt the fear of the unknown or the shyness of meeting and talking to him or her.

As a deafblind Redemptorist priest, my mission to the parishes is to open hope and faith that the deafblind person receives God's message through the kindness of sighted people and that they learn to enjoy the gift of communication with them.

As a deafblind person cannot see nor hear, it all depends on faith, which turns what is unseen and unheard into what is seen and heard through the kindness of communication from sighted persons. This will establish an encounter of joy, hope and trust of God in the lives of the deafblind persons.

Many years before I became totally blind, I used to love going for a long walk in the countryside and watching the wonders of nature – evergreen plants and trees, the wild world full of different colours, the placid lake with ducks swimming on it, the birds flying in the blue sky and so forth. I could not hear the sounds or songs, but I experienced that my sight was God's touch which vibrated throughout my body and spirit.

After becoming totally blind a few years ago, it was an explicit change of my experience in God's touch. Naturally, blindness can be an experience of abandonment or loneliness. But, in fact, the power of God never left me. It transmitted into a different way of seeing God through my senses of smell and touch.

A great amazement came to me when I went for a walk in a lovely garden with many different types of blooming flowers and fresh herbs. The fragrances filled my lungs with a sense of God's power of love. The different shapes of the flower petals and leaves gave me the mystery of God's touch.

At times, the blindness is my lifetime struggle and it leads me to feel down. But through my faith I pursue walking in the garden as it is always uplifting for me because God never abandons us in times when life is changing, like when I lost my sight or hearing.

Sometimes when I cannot go out on account of the weather, I spend time inside holding the holy host – the Body of Christ. I place my hands on it and it signifies my touch on God within my darkness. It is like a stone turning over, turning my inner conflict to inner peace through faith. This gives my imagination an idea of how Jesus touched deafness and blindness. The wealth of touch stays in a human life no matter what comes into our lives. Faith always has an importance to a human being because it knots the bond of trust and faithfulness between God and us.

Faith cannot be seen with a human eye or heard with a human ear, it is simply the wealth of the touch of God without expressing a single word, but connecting with Him with a meaningful spirit.

Fr Cyril Axelrod works from Our Lady of Hal Parish in Camden Town, London.

This article first appeared in *The New Statesman* magazine in April 2008 and is reproduced with permission.

Grace is Everywhere

Abbot Aidan Bellenger OSB

It is not always easy being a priest today. Many of our
contemporaries are suspicious of our motives and ignorant
of our way of life. There has been a massive shift in the
perception of the Catholic priesthood since my childhood
in the 1950s. Then, the priest was honoured in the Catholic
community as a leader and exemplar and portrayed, on T.V.
and film, as a man of quiet integrity or even heroism. Now,
the priest, in the light of the abuse scandals and the dearth
of vocations, is more likely to appear a little isolated even in
his own community and to be presented as a troubled and
sometimes malevolent figure on the screen.

Yet, within the Catholic Church, the priesthood,
in its ministerial aspect, remains crucial to the continuing
vitality of the community. Called to be both the dispenser
of the Sacraments and the preacher of the Word, the
priest is at the heart of the local church. He is an ordained
enabler who, as a helper to the bishop, the successor to
the Apostles, is seen as the spokesman for Christ in his
locality. I am always impressed by the brotherhood and
shared vision of priesthood reflected in such occasions as
the Chrism Mass on Maundy Thursday. Priests come in
all shapes and sizes but they all share the same charisms of
prayer and service.

I was drawn to the priesthood myself by my study
of the past and particularly of the English Recusant
tradition. English Catholics have long experience of being
a minority having to stand up for their rights as well as
preaching the Gospel. We can perhaps today learn much
from the mission-centred mentality of the priests, secular
and religious, called to ministry in the centuries following
the Reformation. Many were martyred and those who
kept their lives often experienced a lifetime of deprivation

and persecution summed up in the phrase "the hunted priest". Yet, famously they retained their very English sense of humour and proportion in the face of hostility, like those Jesuits in 1616 "sitting alone like sparrows upon the housetop, expecting the happy day and the advent of the great God". They can inspire us today by their witness to the mission of the Church and to the centrality of the Mass.

As a monk as well as a priest, I suppose I might be regarded, in modern eyes, as a double anachronism, but what inspired me to be what I became was the life of prayer which made the life of the priest both possible and joyful. In many faiths, and even among some Christians, the priest is a functionary, little more than a ritual official. St Gregory the Great, the sixth century Pope and Apostle of the English, in his wonderful Pastoral Rule, a text book for all called to ministry in the Church, established the principle that the contemplative and the active life have to co-exist and feed each other in the life of the priest.

Working effectively as a priest requires a life of prayer and time for contemplation as well as action. I suspect that if priests could renew their prayer lives their active ministry would benefit greatly. In a world like ours where anxiety and depression can become a way of life then the hope and comfort of prayer is the answer to many problems. A priest as a man of prayer is a strong witness in a doubting world. It will always be a challenge to be a faithful priest but with the enriching spirit of prayer and sacrament it can be a wonderful and fulfilling life.

As a long-term lover of things French I remember re-reading George Bernanos' wonderful *Diary of a Country Priest*, published in 1938, just before my ordination. At one level it is a tragic story of one priest's frustrations and unfulfilled promise. It is not for the faint-hearted. At another, and deeper level, it is about the sanctification of a humble and devoted priest. If, as priests or laity, we are to look around us, we can, alongside the country priest, appreciate that grace is everywhere. In leading our fellow Catholics to understanding the engraced state of our incarnational faith we might discover the core of priesthood.

Abbot Aidan Bellenger OSB, Abbot of Downside Abbey.

To Be With Him

Pope Benedict XVI

"And he appointed twelve, to be with him, and to be sent out" (Mk 3:14).

What exactly are these people being called for? What actually is Jesus' will with regard to them? Two reasons are named: "to be with him" and "to be sent out".

At first glance this seems in fact to be a contradiction. Either, one could say, Jesus wants them to form his entourage and always to accompany him; or he wants people he can send out who then will of course be with him only from time to time. If we transpose this question into the terminology of a later age, then one would say that here the monastic, contemplative vocation and the apostolic vocation seem to be intertwined with each other. We, on the other hand, distinguish them and are of the opinion that to a considerable extent the one excludes the other.

But it is precisely here that Jesus corrects us. Only someone who is with him can be sent, and only someone who lets himself or herself be sent, who transmits his message and his love, is with him. Of course there are various different kinds and forms of this mission, various different patterns of apostolate and of being close to him. I would not want to dispute this here at all. But prior to and transcending all these differences there is a fundamental unity that is indispensable. Apostles are eye-witnesses and, if I may be allowed the term, ear-witnesses. Only someone who knows him, who knows his words and deeds, who has himself or herself experienced him in the encounter of long days and nights – only that kind of person can bring him to others. That is true even today. *"To be with him"* – that is the first and fundamental component of the priestly vocation.

If as a bishop or formerly as a colleague I have looked into the reasons why a vocation which began with so much enthusiasm and so many hopes has gradually collapsed, what emerged was always the same: at some time silent prayer came to a stop – perhaps because of sheer keenness to get on with everything that had to be done. But now the keenness had become just a shell because its inner impetus had been lost. At some time personal confession had come to a halt and with it a contact with challenge and forgiveness, a renewal from within the face of the Lord that is indispensable. "*To be with him*" – this "*with him*" is something one needs not just for a certain initial period so that one could draw on it later. It must always be the core of priestly ministry. But one must practise it and learn it so that in due course it achieves a certain ease and comes to be taken for granted, and thus can be maintained even in difficult times. So I would urge you sincerely to regard this as the fundamental task of your time in the seminary and later of your priestly life: to be with him, to learn to keep your gaze on him, to practise listening to him, to get to know the Lord more and more in prayer and in the patient reading of Holy Scripture.

It is important to cultivate prayer not only when it makes us happy. Just as nothing important in human life can be attained without discipline and method, so too does our inner life need both these. If we listen to a great virtuoso who has a perfect mastery of his or her instrument, we are moved by the ease which simply lets the beauty of the work he or she is playing speak for itself and the relaxed way in which this is apparently taken for granted. But precisely in order for this ease ultimately to exist, in which a masterpiece can be expressed directly and without being masked in any way, a long period of disciplined work is needed beforehand. Our inner life should be no less valuable to us than outward performance, than sport and technical ability. The "growth of the inner person" is worth our entire commitment and effort; the world needs people who have become inwardly mature and rich; the Lord needs them so that he can call them and send them out.

Pope Benedict XVI.

Extract from *Ministers of Your Joy: Reflections on Priestly Spirituality*, published by St Pauls Publishing, 1989.

Learning What it Means to Be a Priest

Fr Vivian Boland OP

The weeks and months after my ordination were anti-climactic. I had reached the goal that had been on the horizon of my life for many years: what now? I began to learn what it means to be a priest from the people who came to see me. They came to talk about difficulties – disappointments, sadness, betrayals, and perplexity of various kinds. They did not necessarily talk immediately or explicitly about the presence and action of God but eventually or implicitly it was always about that. Else why turn to a priest rather than to somebody else?

I found people looking to me to come up with suitable words not only in times of distress but also in times of joy and celebration. I was expected to speak to many different situations, providing words to interpret, comfort, encourage and congratulate. My task, it seemed, was to situate what was happening in a broader and deeper context, to fit the story of this person's life within the Great Story. I began to see it fulfilled, that the priest is first and foremost a man of the word – more truly, of course, a man of the Word since our own words are few, often superficial, and not necessarily those of the wisest person present (a fact I realised quickly and often!). My task, it seemed, was to "preach", to apply the Word of God in particular situations and circumstances, to try to see and show how that Word was being fulfilled in events and experiences.

The words of Scripture and the words of the Liturgy provided the vocabulary I needed. But I realised that these could not simply be quoted cold, that they had to come through me as words that I was myself pondering constantly and using to illuminate the events of my own life. I saw that the spirituality of the priest – once again the theology became flesh – had to be centred on the Bible and the Liturgy if my life was to make any sense. The words of the bishop during the ordination liturgy continue to echo across the years: "model your life after the mystery of the Lord's cross". We contemplate that mystery in the Bible and are taken into it in the Liturgy.

There were many days when very concrete things about the Liturgy were very helpful. Bread and wine are simple but rich. Fruit of the earth but also the work of human hands, they are given a new level of meaning and reality as the bread of life and our spiritual drink. The realities of life, work, family, and friendship – none of this was ever as simple as bread and wine and yet I knew, and encouraged people to know, that everything about us can be brought to the Eucharist and offered there along with the sacrifice of Christ.

The sacrifice is offered "through Him, with Him and in Him", Jesus our priest who gives us the sacrifice to offer and intercedes for ever with the Father. The man who is ordained a priest to represent Christ sacramentally in His offering and in His praying must – to be true to what he is – become like Him in his own service and prayer. Thus many Church documents have focused on the moral and spiritual qualities required of the priest. More recently such documents speak more theologically, inviting priests to understand themselves in relation to the Trinity, to Christ and to the Church.

The work of preaching and presiding reminds me daily that the mysteries of which we are stewards also contain the meaning of that stewardship.

Fr Vivian Boland OP, Socius to the Provincial, and Master of Students at Blackfriars, Oxford.

Thoughts on the Priesthood for the Year of the Priesthood

Seán Cardinal Brady

As Rector of the Irish College in Rome, I often marvelled at the ability of the Holy Spirit to inspire the hearts of men from so many different countries and such a wide variety of gifts, interests and personalities to the priesthood. It was always an inspiration to witness their generosity, enthusiasm and commitment as they approached the day of their ordination. It left me in no doubt about the appeal of the Gospel to every generation and that the Lord is constant in seeking out generous servants of God's people, pastors after his own heart.

Today when I meet priests from across the world they all tell me the same thing: "I have never been busier". The priest is still in constant demand. The harvest is still rich. People of all backgrounds and with all sorts of needs, difficulties and questions still look to the Catholic priest as a unique and accessible source of spiritual, moral and charitable service and as a universal symbol of God's presence in the world. As one of my friends never tires repeating, "the priest is a wanted man".

Often the impact of this priestly ministry is quiet, lived out in service of the every day needs of people and their lives. At other times it is dramatic, even heroic. I think for example of Fr Ragheed Ganni, a young priest of the Chaldean Catholic Church who spent his last years of post-graduate study in the Irish College in Rome. When I met him there from time to time I was always struck by his obvious joy at being a priest. While he loved the sights and sounds of Rome, as well as travelling around Europe during the student holidays, he was determined to complete his studies so that he could return to his home Diocese of Mosul in Iraq. This was in spite of the threats to the Christian community there following the

U.S. occupation of Iraq in 2003. "That is where I belong, that is my place", he would say. Then shortly after returning home, in an interview for Asia News about the war in Iraq, he said something which brings us to the very heart of the Catholic priesthood and its vital importance to the whole people of God: "Without Sunday", he explained, "without the Eucharist, the Christians in Iraq cannot survive."

He was right. Without the Eucharist, the Church cannot survive. Without the priesthood, there can be no Eucharist.

Only a short time later, in June 2007, Fr Ragheed, aged only thirty-five, was slain, shot dead in his car along with three deacons after celebrating Mass for a fearful and persecuted Christian community in his parish Church of the Holy Spirit in Mosul. As I remember him, as I remember his joy, his courage and his selfless generosity, I am reminded of the quiet heroism of so many priests across the world. I am reminded of Fr Manuel Musallam, the Parish Priest of Gaza, whom I had the privilege to visit in his parish last year. Although pastor to a very small Catholic community in the middle of Gaza, he runs one of the largest schools and a vitally needed Catholic Hospital in Gaza City. Despite the many human deprivations of living in the midst of this most difficult part of the world, he works tirelessly in service of the local Muslim and Christian community, responding to their human needs, acting as peace-maker, reconciler, morale booster and spiritual guide. I think of priests like the late Mgr Denis Faul and others here in Ireland who played such a vital role in the peace process here. I think of Fr Hugh Mullan and Fr Noel Fitzpatrick, two priests who were shot dead in Belfast during the early part of the troubles in Northern Ireland while administering the sacrament of the sick to children and others who had been shot. I am reminded of the ultimate joy of the priest, the ultimate service he offers to the people of God in making our Lord present in the Eucharist in the midst of all their needs.

The Eucharist, the source and summit of the Church's activity, the fountain from which all her power flows, remains the most vital and the most privileged part of the ministry of a Catholic priest. It has always been by returning to this essential link between the Priesthood and the Eucharist that my own appreciation of the privilege of being a priest has been renewed.

As we set out on this Year of the Priesthood, a wonderful and timely initiative of Pope Benedict XVI, my prayer is that every priest will rediscover the joy and privilege of being a priest. I pray that solidarity between priests in every diocese and across the world will be renewed and deepened. We need that solidarity with each other and with the people of God to keep our ministry fresh and our human needs supported. We need to remain close to Jesus in prayer, so that what we say and do as priests will come, not from us, but from his presence in us, and through us bring his life to the world.

In a world that yearns for hope, the ministry of the Catholic priest continues to be vital. Indeed, it has never been more urgent or necessary. We are bearers of hope, a hope – as St Paul reminds us – that will not be confounded. We are ambassadors of the kingdom of God and artisans of the civilisation of love. We are heralds of the Gospel and ministers of the healing, restoring and renewing grace of God. The world yearns for this healing, this hope and this grace which the ministry of the priesthood brings.

It is a wonderful privilege to be a priest. It is an even greater privilege to serve Christ and his people. When we do so with generosity and joy, like Fr Ragheed and so many others, then men will be inspired to follow in our path and to give their lives in generous service of God's people in the unique and vital ministry of the priest.

Seán Cardinal Brady, Archbishop of Armagh.

We Can't Give
What We Haven't First Received

Fr Jim Brand

Generous people enjoy giving but are maybe slow to receive. I presume all who are priests or attracted to the priesthood are generous people. In eternity the Father has given everything to the Son. By receiving all, the Son has given the Father the gift of being able to give. There is nothing more frustrating than to want to give and no one will receive. Our Lord felt this when he wept over Jerusalem. In the Trinity the giving and receiving have equal dignity, but in this world we tend to canonise the givers and patronise the receivers. The Father specialises in giving and when we receive our gifts and our unique being the Father is able to be at his best. The Son specialises in forgiving, so when we accept forgiveness we have made the Son happy and there is rejoicing in heaven. The Father will say to us "Thank you for allowing me to love you," and the Son says "Thank you for allowing me to forgive you". Mary was looked on in her nothingness, but by receiving all, she gave the Father the gift of the Incarnation of the Son. We are nothing of ourselves, but he who is mighty has done great things for us.

Exhaustion is the great problem of priests and generous people. We live in a world that gives credit for our doings and not for our being. "*Agere sequitur esse* – our being follows from our doing." If we think we are slaves we will behave like slaves, but if we remember we are princes and princesses in the Kingdom, we will live with joy and freedom as part of the Divine Family. God IS in eternity, but as far as we know God has only DONE in the last 14000 million years, if you believe the Big Bang theory. What is important is WHO we are not just what we do. The Church tends to emphasise the Martha in us, our achievements, which can make us competitive. Daisies don't have breakdowns; they just flower, and we have been sent to bloom. That serenity is catching. Some priests make others seasick in the wash they generate by their busyness. You remember Mary sat and Martha was always busy. Each of us is both Martha and Mary. If we're all Mary we die of starvation and if all Martha we die of exhaustion. Being and doing work together.

Many priests suffer from self-neglect. They are diffident about the wonder of their being. We must remember that we are all unique characters and our first gift from God is our BEING which we are invited to own and cherish. The value of our work is first of all not WHAT we do but WHO is doing it.

One cause of exhaustion is having to deal with many people's different expectations of us. I suggest we are sent to preach the Gospel and the Church's teaching, whatever difficulties we may have ourselves with some of the teachings. People have a right to beautiful Sacraments, to my prayer for them and to reasonable pastoral access. Some priests from their generosity live without brakes, a danger to themselves and to everyone else. One reason some priests don't stop work is that they have no interests and don't take time for friends. How can we preach about love when we have no one to love? The priesthood is NOT meant to be a lonely life. It is filled with love and affection and humour. But sometimes we have to deal with suffering and distress. All the more reason for healthy relationships, contemplative prayer when the still waters run deep and creative use of the body through exercise, music, hobbies, sport.

That is what we are ordained for; anything else is a bonus. With a joyful heart do the Lord's work with a generous spirit but make sure you receive more than you give as IT IS IN RECEIVING THAT WE GIVE.

Fr Jim Brand, Parish Priest of Chorleywood, Hertfordshire.

Priesthood

Bishop Tom Burns SM

I came up behind another car on the motorway and couldn't help but notice that the rear windscreen was plastered with stickers. You know the type of thing: *Baby on board. Child in car.* And even: *Mother-in-law in boot!* But below this, stretched across the full width of the rear window, was a sticker that particularly caught my eye. It read: *Be patient with me. God hasn't finished making me yet.* Now, those sentiments come from Tertullian, our earliest Christian historian, in the third century AD. And he also said something else related to this: *Christians are made, not born.* In other words, making us Christian is not something that is finished at the moment we are born. Making us priests is not something that is finished at the moment we are baptised – or even ordained. It is something that we have to work at throughout our lives. We didn't learn to swim overnight, or drive a car, or gain qualifications in specialist areas, without years of training and effort. *God made me*, said the catechism. Well: *No, he didn't.* A more correct translation would be: *God made me – and goes on making me.* His work is not yet finished. So it is with priesthood. God makes us every day. His grace introduces us to new experiences of himself each and every day. We grow into his ways and his life in every moment that we turn to him – and find that he is already turned to us, waiting, smiling, laughing at our plans!

Never give up, even when we feel helpless, or we have nothing else to give. Always keep in mind that: *When we are down to nothing, God is up to something.* Somewhere deep down inside us, we know that if we let God into what is going on, we will have to change, and if we find it so difficult to change ourselves, imagine how difficult it is to change other people. Behold conversion! For that is precisely what we are talking about. It is not a single, dramatic event. There might not be a blinding light, as happened to St Paul on the road to Damascus – or as one kid wrote in an essay: *on the road to Domestos!* Conversion requires a leap of faith, a leap into the unknown. Yet, it is not a leap across just *one* gigantic chasm, after which the going is straightforward. It is more like the journey across a glacier, as described by Sir Edmund Hillary, one of my childhood heroes, who attempted the impossible without the training, the technology, or the equipment that became essential to others who accepted the same challenge after him. In his book: *The Ascent of Everest*, he sets out a wise policy:

> We approached a shallow gully split from side to side by gaping crevasses. The area was in constant and audible movement. No day passed without some striking change occurring, calling for a fresh reconnaissance of the route.

Any journey of faith for us as priests involves facing many an abyss over and over again, in unpredictable places, and without warning, and obliging us to find new routes to the same goal. It is not a matter of finding grounds for faith, so much as finding faith when the ground disappears.

How do we do that? Well, King George VI gave one answer, in his Christmas Day broadcast in 1939, he quoted a little-known poet called Minnie Louise Haskins. She said:

> … put your hand into the hand of God.
> That shall be better than light
> and safer than a known way!

Go out into the unknown. Oh, how as priests we so often fear uncertainty. Oh, how we are reluctant to LET GO! LET GOD! to let go of what we've always known, to move on from familiar ways. Can we let go of even feeling hurt and rejected? The hardest ministry of all is to let God do in us what we dare not even think of. But it will make all the difference – to us and to others.

Bishop Tom Burns SM, Bishop of Menevia.

Reflections on Priesthood

Bishop Michael Campbell OSA

I have always believed that priesthood is a most precious gift of Christ to his Church, a theme that the late Pope John Paul II often reflected upon, especially in his regular Holy Thursday messages to priests. Each one of us at some time in our own journey of faith has reason to be grateful for the presence and ministry of at least one good priest. Our sense of faith assures us in these moments that there is Another active and at work through the ministry of such priests, Christ himself.

The long tradition and firm teaching of the Church declares that Christ, the supreme high priest himself, intended the saving work he accomplished through his passion, death and resurrection to continue and to be made accessible to people of every generation. Central to Christ's purpose would be the role of the ministerial priesthood, begun with the apostles and mediated through their successors, the college of bishops, and their helpers, priests and deacons. In sacramental language, the Church has come to understand and describe this ministry as Holy Orders.

For obvious reasons, therefore, a very close bond has always existed between priesthood and the holy Eucharist, the sacrifice of the Mass. Christ's command to his apostles to re-enact the Last Supper in his memory is one that the Church has faithfully observed through the ministry of her priests from the very outset. The rich Catholic teaching on the Eucharist derives from the conviction that in these sacred elements Christ is uniquely present among his people, feeding and nourishing them. In this salvific encounter between Christ and his bride, the Church, the role of the priest is central. We can see why in Catholic piety the priest has often been called "*alter Christus*", another Christ.

The Church cannot but be subject to the ebb and flow of historical change. Her self-understanding and theological outlook tend to be conditioned by the age in which she finds herself. The perception and role of the ministry of priests will consequently reflect the particular historical circumstances of the day. Some Catholics today can be disconcerted by an apparent change of emphasis as to what precisely a priest's function might be, and so we witness the phenomenon of so-called liberal versus conservative among some elements of the clergy. Yet surely the essence of priesthood remains at heart constant and unchanging: to proclaim the gospel of Christ and make accessible to his people the fruits of his redemption primarily through the sacrament of his body and blood.

My own experience of priestly ministry over many years as a religious priest has been varied but always fulfilling. Whether teaching in schools or seminary, chaplaincy work or that of parish priest, I have always felt content in what I was doing, and as the years pass with a growing sense of being deeply privileged to share in the lives of a large number of God's people. Aware that we are merely servants of Christ, as the apostle Paul puts it, nevertheless the affection and the appreciation on the part of so many is both touching and humbling. It is on such occasions that we grasp, albeit dimly, that there has to be someone else shadowing us and enhancing our efforts in a mysterious way, and this is a tangible reminder of Christ's promise that he would be with us for all time.

In the course of the Church's long history, the office of priesthood has been assumed by quite remarkable and different characters. In the months ahead the Church will observe the one hundred and fiftieth anniversary of the death of that outstanding model for every priest, St John Vianney, the Curé of Ars. The witness of his life and priestly dedication continues to inspire and encourage those of us who live in times and circumstances so different from his. Yet this humble priest's persevering commitment to prayer, love of his people, and trust in God yielded a harvest which not even he could have dreamed of. Although St John Vianney was indeed unique as a priest, many other inspiring examples of priestly figures from every epoch of Church history could be cited.

The rapidly changing modern world in which we live poses many challenges to our understanding of the role of priesthood in our Church. As a religious priest and bishop, I find consolation and reassurance in the distinguished line of bishops, priests and deacons who have preceded us in the long life of the Church, not least in the wonderful patron of the Order to which I belong, St Augustine of Hippo. Many have been truly outstanding and their names are known to us, countless others laboured quietly and anonymously and are known to God alone. As part of that splendid priestly tradition they continue to speak to us, urging us on to continue running in the race we have started. With such a great cloud of witnesses surrounding us …let us run the race which stretches before us, (Heb 12:1).

Bishop Michael Campbell OSA, Bishop of Lancaster.

The Carthusian

A Carthusian

"A very precious way to pray is just through silence. No thoughts or words, just wanting to be silent in the presence of God. Perhaps one of the high points in prayer is where two silences meet: God's silence and our silence. No need for thoughts – and words get in the way."

Cardinal Basil Hume OSB, *Mystery of Love*

All are called to holiness, to be holy as God is holy, that is our human dignity and grace. But some few are called to follow a less frequented path to achieve it. Not because of any merit on their part, but to fulfil a particular function in the Church; in the case of the solitary, to witness visibly, in his life, to the absolute priority of God over any created thing.

Christ looks at someone, loves him and invites him to leave everything he has and to follow Him in his radical surrender to God and in His mission for the salvation of mankind.

"By penance, we have our part in the saving work of Christ, who redeemed the human race from the oppressive bondage of sin, above all by pouring forth prayer to the Father and by offering himself to him in sacrifice. Thus it comes about that we, too, even though we abstain from exterior activity, exercise nevertheless an apostolate of a very high order, since we strive to follow Christ in this, the inmost heart of his saving task." (Statutes, 34.4) This is the essential priesthood of the Carthusian: the cloister monks also exercise a more ministerial role within the cloister.

On the occasion of the ordination of two young men within the Carthusian Order, one of the Fathers present wrote these lines asking us to consider these few passages taken from the Statutes of the Order:

"If therefore we are truly living in union with God, our minds and hearts, far from becoming shut in on themselves, open up to embrace the whole universe and the mystery of Christ that saves it. Apart from all, to all we are united, so that it is in the name of all that we stand before the living God. This continual effort to be always – as far as human frailty permits – very close to God, unites us in a special way with the Blessed Virgin Mary, whom we are accustomed to call the Mother, in particular, of all Carthusians." (34.2)

"Wherefore in praise of God – for which the hermit Order of Carthusians was founded in a special way – let us dedicate ourselves to the peace and silence of our cells and strive to offer Him unceasing worship, so that, sanctified in truth, we may be those true worshippers whom the Father seeks." (34.5)

"Let the Fathers keep in mind the close union in Christ that they have with the Brothers, and remember that it is thanks to them that they are enabled to offer pure prayer to the Lord in the peace and solitude of their cells: let them remember too that their priesthood is for the service of the Church and in particular of those members close to them, namely the Brothers in their community." (3:5)

"All this finds its source and support in the celebration of the Eucharistic sacrifice, which is the efficacious sign of unity. It is also the centre and high point of our life, as well as the spiritual food for our exodus in solitude, by which through Christ we return to the Father. Throughout the entire liturgical cycle, Christ prays both for us as our Priest and in us as our Head; hence it is that we may hear our voices in Him and His in us." (3:7)

Compiled with the help of a Carthusian from St Hugh's Charterhouse, Parkminster, West Sussex.

The Priesthood Beyond Repression

Archbishop Mark Coleridge

Pope Benedict has announced that there is to be a special Year of the Priesthood or, better perhaps, a Year of the Priest. This will coincide with the 150th anniversary of the death of St John Vianney, the Curé of Ars who is patron saint of parish priests.

Twenty years ago I visited Ars, more out of a sense of duty than enthusiasm. Yet when I got there and walked through his little house and knelt in the basilica where he lies, I found it all strangely moving, even haunting. It struck deep chords in me, as John Vianney has done for so long in the heart of the Church.

Yet in many ways the Curé of Ars can seem very alien to us 150 years after his death. However, as a friend of mine said recently, "I like the alien: it speaks of what we repress." That is true, I think; and it led me to ask, what do we find alien about John Vianney? Which is to ask, what is it that we repress, or at least tend to forget, about the priesthood? What are those things to which the Curé of Ars stands as enduring witness, even if we tend to forget them? I point to three.

The first is *mediation*. John Vianney had a profound sense of himself as a man called and set apart to represent God to human beings and human beings to God – never more so than at the altar and in the confessional. This presumes an intimate knowledge of both God and the human being, and these we see in him to an extraordinary degree. Talk of the priest as mediator can stir fear that the priest will be too separate, too "other" – especially perhaps in a country like Australia where one of the greatest strengths of the priesthood has been the closeness of priests to people. It can sound clericalist to speak of the priest as a mediating figure who is separate or other. Yet the otherness we see in John Vianney is a way of becoming unusually close to people; it is a way of intimacy. It is a way of living the strange intimacy of Christ himself, his unique closeness to the Church and the world.

The second point at which the Curé of Ars can seem alien is *mercy*. Here I mean not just the human comfort which pastors offer so well in so many situations. I mean the overwhelming mercy of God. In John Vianney, this led to a horror of sin, which is why he often wept at the stories of sin he heard in the confessional. One of the great prayers of Lent is that we may never grow used to sin. To this we might also add that we may grow more and more in a sense of the power and beauty of God's mercy. It was this sense that led John Vianney to spend hours a day in the confessional – as much as eighteen hours later in his life as thousands came to seek God's mercy from him in the Sacrament. I ask, therefore, if we need a renaissance of the Sacrament of Reconciliation. I think we do. We need a resurgence of the sense of the horror of sin and the glory of mercy, beginning with the priests. This may be one of our greatest tasks in this Year of the Priest and one of its greatest legacies.

At the third of the points, the Curé of Ars can seem most alien of all. It is *mortification*. Even the word sounds alien in a world which sees mortification of the flesh as a denial of the body, implying that the flesh is bad, which is unacceptable for Christians who profess faith in the Incarnation and the resurrection of the body. John Vianney undertook throughout his life a tough regime of bodily mortification, but not as a rejection of the flesh. For him, asceticism was a way of affirming the truth and beauty of the flesh which are discovered only when the flesh is set in harmony with the spirit. In a world that tends to say that there is only the flesh, it is a counter-cultural way of saying that there is more than the flesh. Mortification, it has been said, is also a uniquely powerful way to unsettle the demons of softness, pessimism and lukewarm faith. It is a way of feeding faith, hope and love.

John Vianney lived in a world where there were many false dawns. After the French Revolution there were other revolutions, each with its own great promise and each unleashing only another tide of blood. Yet in that human desert there was a wholly unexpected flourishing of grace, of which John Vianney was so brilliant a part, as were figures like Marcellin Champagnat, Peter Julian Eymard, Bernadette Soubirous and Thérèse Martin, the Little Flower. It was a great eruption of the supernatural in an unlikely time, a sign of the true revolution, the revolution of God's grace. The supernatural, the grace, is love. The love has a name and a face; and the name and the face are Jesus. It is he whom we see in the strange little figure of the Curé of Ars; and that is why John Vianney remains as fresh as tomorrow, however alien he may seem at first sight. It is the same Jesus we see somehow in every man ordained as priest, which is why the Catholic priesthood will always be strange, new and necessary.

Archbishop Mark Coleridge, Archbishop of Canberra and Goulburn.

The Priest as Confessor

Canon Daniel Cronin

I remember very well Cardinal Hume once saying to us: "I wish people would go to confession more often, not so much for their own sakes, but for the benefit of the priests who hear those confessions." I think what Cardinal Basil was trying to convey is summarised in this beautiful and profound extract from an article written some years ago for the *The Mulberry* magazine published by our seminary at Allen Hall, in Chelsea. The author and a fellow contributor to this book is Fr John Farrell OP, currently Prior Provincial of the Dominican Friars in Great Britain; he wrote:

> In confession you hear what only the Almighty
> should hear.
> Like God, as they stumble out their sins and
> omissions,
> you hear the goodness that they are not aware of,
> and are humbled.
> Like God, you find them, as they do not find
> themselves,
> lovable, touchingly lovable.

Yes, indeed, whilst celebrating that sacrament *in persona Christi*, I have frequently been humbled but also immensely edified by the humility and openness of people who want to "entrust their past to the mercy of God, the present to his love and the future to his providence" (St Augustine).

On more occasions than I care to remember, people have said to me that it must be such a burden to sit listening to other people pouring out their life and concerns to you hour after hour. For some years I unthinkingly went along with that assessment. In fact it is not like that at all. For fifteen years I spent at least a few hours every week hearing confessions in Westminster Cathedral where I discovered what a precious sacrament it is. The privilege of being used by Our Lord as a conduit of grace where one could lift the crippling burdens and past heavy baggage from people's lives is indeed reminiscent of being a doctor of the soul. To witness the weight of unhealthy guilt being lifted from the shoulders of a penitent is a truly wonderful experience. As someone once said: "I came expecting punishment and what I received was God's mercy."

Not that hearing confessions is all heavy duty listening. It is true that what we hear in this sacrament must go with us to our graves. However there is one little amusing vignette I can share, because it is not strictly confessional material, and in any case the lady involved gave me her full permission to share what she said as it made me laugh so much. This good lady came in to tell me that she was visiting from Ireland, and the conversation went like this, though the story would be far better if I could tell it by audio means, but please try to imagine an accent which hailed from the Kingdom of Kerry: "Well, Father, my husband and I have been over here from Ireland on holiday in London, and didn't my husband take a heart attack on me in Victoria Street, and listen here to me, didn't he die on me. Father, would you ever remember him in your prayers?" Of course I said that I would. She then paused for a few seconds and said: "Yerra, Father, if you forgot, I wouldn't hold it against you!" I am not entirely sure to this day whether that reflected more on her relationship with her husband or a beautiful understanding of forgetful priests.

One experience I have never forgotten was helping out on a Ministry to Priests retreat in Glasgow which ended with a very moving Penitential Service where all of us priests had the chance of availing ourselves of the sacrament of reconciliation. If I recall correctly the service was presided over by Cardinal Tom Winning who gave us a unique and refreshing penance. He told us that we who so often said

Masses for other people, but never for ourselves, were to say a Mass for our own intentions. If you are a priest, please do that for yourself, and if you are not, perhaps it might be a kindness to have a Mass said for the intentions of your own parish priest.

Canon Daniel Cronin, Canon of Westminster Cathedral and Parish Priest of St Thomas More, Knebworth, Hertfordshire.

Inhabiting the Word

Bishop John Crowley

In my early years within the Diocese of Middlesbrough I used to go for spiritual guidance to a much loved member of the Ampleforth Benedictine Community, Father Ian Petit. At the time, he was stationed with three other monks at Osmotherley, responsible both for the parish and for the ancient shrine of Our Lady of Mount Grace. It was a joy to meet with him – his warmth of manner, good humour and compassionate spiritual wisdom made Father Ian the ideal director for me and many others. His death left a gap which was difficult to fill.

I remember on one occasion pouring out a lengthy *"woe is me"* tale after a particularly testing period of diocesan leadership. He listened carefully as usual – empathetic understanding was a lovely gift of his, allied to a ready appreciation of the struggles of the human heart – and then offered some advice which has remained with me to this day. *"There are times* (he said) *when the going becomes more than usually rough and tough, and then it is a question of hanging on in there until the storms blow over. But then* (he added) – and this is the word of wisdom which has remained steadily in my memory-bank – *it is all the more vital at such times to 'inhabit the promises'. By these, I mean those occasions in the gospels where Jesus makes a rock solid commitment to be at our side."* ...

> "Come to me, all you who labour and are overburdened, and I will give you rest. Shoulder my yoke and learn from me, for I am gentle and humble in heart, and you will find rest for your souls. Yes, my yoke is easy and my burden light" (Mt 11:28-30).

43

"I am with you always, yes, until the end of time" (Mt 28:20).

"I am the vine, you are the branches. Whoever remains in me, with me in him, will bear fruit in plenty" (Jn 15:5).

"I have come so that you may have life and have it to the full" (Jn 10:10).

But Ian Petit didn't just point me towards such life-giving words. He did something else too, he urged me to *"inhabit"* them. He reminded me, in fact, that such promises given by Truth Himself remain only words on a printed page unless they are taken down to heart level. So, for the next few minutes, dear reader, I would invite you to read through those promises again quite slowly, and pausing in between each one. Let me encourage you to *breathe* them in and to *inhabit* them in the depth of your being.

Bishop John Crowley, Bishop Emeritus of Middlesbrough.

Maasai Apostolate

Mgr John Dale

I remember the moment very clearly. Bishop Holland grabbed my lapel and whispered into my ear, "I want you to go to Africa!"

1983, seven years ordained and a whole new world was opening up for me. There wasn't much doubt in my heart about whether to say "Yes" but it took a few weeks for my mind to become accustomed to the idea. Africa. The missions. Maasai. Me. Gosh!

I had long harboured a love for the missions; ever since my schooldays when Mother Rose used to tell me of her years in Borneo, and the White Fathers entranced me with their tales. Later, as a priest, I enjoyed having the Mission Appeal priests in the parish – especially the older ones who had borne the heat of the day. Now it was my turn!

There were few illusions about the challenge. I would have to learn at least one new language, adapt to different social and church cultures; for some time I would be a fish out of water. I would miss family and friends and it would be a wrench to leave the parish where I was so settled but … I was thirty-one years old with plenty of energy and enthusiasm, and so the journey began.

My experience in Kenya was very life-giving and way beyond anything I could have imagined. It was almost like learning to be a priest again, but with a much broader focus.

Working with "professional" missionaries was stimulating. These men and women had a specific charism, a different training; they even understood missiology! I respected them as the inheritors of the tradition begun by holy founders such as Cardinal Vaughan and Alice Ingham. However, more than anything, I appreciated their hospitality – relief from dusty roads and the struggles of communicating in an alien culture. This was matched by the welcome extended by the local people; their kindness during the great famine of '84 and '85 was almost painful to accept.

Enormously impressive was the huge responsibility taken by catechists and lay leaders. Parish Councils were virtually unknown in 1983 in Salford but here they were the norm. Men and women were running the Church and not simply in the absence of a priest. Small Christian Communities took responsibility for pastoral care and formation of local worshipping communities. This was very exciting.

As I look back however, I reflect that the greatest impact was made by the breadth of liturgical expression I encountered. The music and dance throughout the Mass, and especially at the offertory procession, were an exuberant expression of people's relationship with their Creator. Traditional tunes and rhythms familiar to them from childhood were adapted, incorporating prayers and hymns used all over the world.

On the way back from Kenya, completing my five year loan period, I stayed in Rome for a few days. It was the first time I had been there and so was staggered by the sense of history particularly in the monumental buildings. Coming straight from an African culture where history is expressed in oral traditions and customs rather than bricks and mortar, I was dumbfounded. The contrast was immense and my sense of Catholicity stretched rather than expanded.

I felt ill at ease when I visited St Peter's Basilica; the size was almost impossible to comprehend. The footprint of just one of its twelve massive columns was bigger than each of the three wooden chapels I had built in the parish. I had to struggle with conflicting emotions. I didn't know if I was angry, disappointed, overawed or just overwhelmed.

Having been back to St Peter's and Kenya several times since – twenty years older – I now have a broader perspective. I know both expressions of the Church are valid but I remember the African Church with huge affection and admiration for its simplicity and enthusiasm.

So I am enormously glad to be back in 'the missions' helping provide continuing support for the new and developing churches of Africa and Asia through **Missio**.

Monsignor John Dale, a priest of Salford Diocese, is the National Director of **Missio** – the Pontifical Mission Societies.

The Priest "Another Christ"

Cahal Cardinal Daly

Every Christian is called to be "another Christ". That is why we are called Christians: "Christian" means "Christ-person". Each Christian is a person who is called to live like Christ, to love like Christ, to *be* like Christ. Others should thus see in her or him some reflection of what Jesus Christ is like. We could speak of Christian living as a process of Christification. The priest can in a special way be called "another Christ".

Christification is the work of the sacraments in our lives: the sacraments are Jesus Christ himself, through the power of the Holy Spirit, gradually and progressively transforming our human nature into the being of Christ, so that increasingly it is Christ himself who thinks in us, speaks in us, loves in us, forgives in us; it is Christ who lives in us.

For the priest, this absorption into Christ is most powerfully effected in the celebration of the Eucharist. When the priest pronounces the words of consecration in the Mass, he uses the very words of Christ himself as if they were his own words: "This is my body… This is my blood". This is an awesome reality, particularly for the priest.

Similarly, in the sacrament of reconciliation, the priest says to the penitent:

> "I absolve you from your sins
> in the name of the Father, and of the Son,
> and of the Holy Spirit."

These words too are dramatic. They too are awesome. No one can forgive sins but God alone, and yet we priests find ourselves saying to a penitent, "I absolve you". We cannot but be amazed at what we are doing and saying. In order to extend his mercy to sinners, God allows another sinner, the priest, to act and to speak in his Divine and Holy Name, and gives to his priests the power to do what only the All-Holy God can do and say.

In the sacraments the priest acts in the person of Christ, (*in persona Christi*). To do this authentically the priest must be familiar with Jesus Christ as foretold in the Old Testament and revealed in the New. The priest must be a man of Scripture. He must make the prayerful reading of Holy Scripture a central feature of his life. "Ignorance of scripture is ignorance of Christ", said St Jerome. Familiarity with Scripture is familiarity with Christ.

Our preaching must be based on Holy Scripture. It must be applied to the real human and social situations with which people are confronted. But the primary aim of preaching must be the development in our listeners of a personal relationship with Jesus Christ, a relationship which inspires people to view the opportunities and the challenges of modern living through the eyes of Christ and to respond to them as Christ would respond. In short, good preaching is the result of holiness in the preacher, and has for its purpose the fostering of holiness among the hearers. Calls for renewal in the Church often concentrate on the need for renewal of its institutions. This is indeed an ongoing task, but the primary renewal of the Church is the call to holiness of all its members, lay people and priests. Without this, no renewal will succeed.

Personal holiness can come to be seen as being in contrast with pastoral effectiveness. The example of Christ himself shows how false that contrast is. Jesus is repeatedly shown in the Gospels as taking the disciples apart with him to a place where they could be alone and pray. When the priest is praying he is still serving his people, praying for them and at the same time making himself more "fit for purpose" in the service he gives his people

There is no holiness without prayer. It is a primary obligation for a priest to be a man of prayer. He must be someone who, by his own example, inspires people to pray. The disciples ask Jesus: "Teach us to pray". The priest must be one who, out of his own personal experience, can teach his people to pray. The best way to learn to pray is to pray. The best qualification for a teacher of prayer is to be a person of prayer.

After sixty-eight years of priesthood, I can only praise and thank the Lord for the privilege and the happiness in priestly service which he has given to me. I have often felt "cast down" at my unworthiness and failures, but I have been uplifted again by trust in God's mercy. I find I can express my feelings best in the words of Psalm 42, which we used to recite at the beginning of the Latin Mass in pre-Vatican Council days:

> "I will come to the altar of God,
> the God of my joy.
> My redeemer, I will thank you on the harp,
> O God, my God.
>
> Why are you cast down, my soul,
> why groan within me?
> Hope in God; I will praise him still,
> my Saviour and my God."

Cahal Cardinal Daly, Archbishop Emeritus of Armagh.

The Fire of the Holy Spirit

Daniel Cardinal DiNardo

I have always loved the Fathers of the Church and have studied them both formally at the Augustinianum in Rome and informally in my preparations for homilies. St John Chrysostom is one of the few Fathers to have written a book on the priesthood. It has rightfully become famous and gives us some wonderful insight into the Sacrament of Holy Orders. At one point he compares the work of the priest with the Prophet Elias who called down fire upon a sacrifice he had prepared so that it would be consumed and thus become a sign for the faith of Israel which had grown cold. St John Chrysostom then writes: "Pass from there to the sacrifice that is offered now… For the priest stands bringing down not fire, but the Holy Spirit and he prays long not that fire may descend from heaven and consume the oblation, but that grace may descend upon the victim, and through it inflame the souls of all and render them brighter than silver tried by fire…"

This early beautiful description of the priest as the guardian and custodian of the "epiclesis," of the calling down and invoking of the Holy Spirit, a call done in complete humility and modesty, but with authority, has always struck me as a significant point for understanding the mystery of the priesthood. The mystery of the epiclesis is most intense at the Eucharist and in the Eucharistic Prayer, the heart of the Liturgy and of the priest's life. The priest must be and is a humble man, a sinner called by the Lord in Baptism and called anew for the work of communion in the Church as a priest. He must be soaked in prayer begging the Advocate to take hold of himself and his priestly work so that the Church may be enlarged in spirit and be set on fire with the love of God and neighbour. I hope and pray that every priest will be suffused with this fire and love of the Gift of the Father and his Well-Beloved Son, the Gift of the Holy Spirit.

Daniel Cardinal DiNardo, Archbishop of Galveston-Houston.

The Variety of Priestly Ministry

Fr Brian Doolan

Each morning when I wake up I thank God for the gift of a new day and for the gift of faith. Faith makes life worth living and means that each day is an opportunity to discover afresh God's love and goodness and mercy. Each day, too, I thank God for the gift of the priesthood which he has entrusted to me. Because through my ministry as a priest my own faith is constantly strengthened and renewed and I am able to celebrate it and share it with my parishioners. Each day brings unique and wonderful experiences of seeing Christ at work in the lives of men and women. For me the daily round of prayer, especially the Office, and the Mass, is the opportunity to keep in touch with God and to receive the grace and help I need to live the life of Christ. The daily encounter with the Word of God in word and sacrament is truly life-giving and gives me energy and inspiration.

Each day brings a wide variety of encounters with people. For eight years I was Dean of St Chad's Cathedral in Birmingham and in contact with the hundreds of people who came to the Cathedral to worship and pray and as tourists and visitors, as well as the large numbers of students who took part in the schools programme. It was a constant round of new faces and immediate pastoral demands. The Cathedral is a major heritage asset and it was always my concern to help the visitors become pilgrims, to meet the Lord and be touched by him. That is the essential difference between being a curator and a Dean. There was always the round of diocesan Masses and ceremonies. In my lesser moments I sometimes felt that I was a cross between a theatre stage manager and a circus entrepreneur. But this too is part of the Church's ministry and a source of inspiration because of the evident joy of those who came to them.

For the past two years I have been parish priest of a scattered rural parish in south Warwickshire with three small and beautiful churches. The physical contrast from Birmingham's city centre could hardly be greater. Now, whenever I leave the presbytery, I meet people I know. I can visit my parishioners, spend time with them and share the life of a stable and vibrant community of faith, and through my pastoral ministry I am daily made aware of the goodness and mercy and power of God working in peoples' lives. It is this which makes the life of the priest such a joy.

The wonderful variety of priestly life is one of its greatest attractions. No two parishes are the same and no two days are the same and there is the opportunity to use what gifts and talents God has given me to the full. The struggles and sacrifices are as real and challenging for me as for every priest. But struggle and sacrifice are part of being human and there is always the hope and glory of the Cross through which we are redeemed. I am not sure why God wanted me to be a priest. I am not worthy of such a privilege but I constantly thank him that he does want me and that he continues to inspire me with love for him and his people. It has given me the best and most enriching life that I could imagine. I would not want to change it for anything else.

Fr Brian Doolan, Parish Priest of Our Lady & the Apostles, Brailes.

Journeying Together Along the Road of God's Calling

Bishop Terence Drainey

"The harvest is rich but the labourers are few, so ask the Lord of the harvest to send labourers to his harvest. I am sending you out like lambs among wolves. Say to all you meet, 'The Kingdom of God is very near you'." (Lk 10:2,4,10)

Each of us is called to fulfil our part in God's plan for providing labourers in his harvest of salvation, and we also are called to proclaim this same message of salvation. Both sound rather daunting faced with our present climate of apparent hostility to the Gospel and antipathy to the mission of the Church. What can we do about it? The problem is well beyond us, surely!

I have been very blessed in my ministry as a priest and now as a bishop. I have had so many wonderful opportunities to recognise God's hand at work in my life and the lives of those to whom I have ministered. I have always been surrounded by good and encouraging people right from the first beginnings in the heart of my family and home community. These are the places where I first learned about the Kingdom of God being very near. I don't think anyone ever used that expression; in fact, I am very sure they didn't, but this is where I took it all in, almost by osmosis, because that was what my family, friends and others around me were living. This is where I first felt that the Lord of the harvest was calling me to come and labour in his harvest. Again, I don't think anyone used that expression, but in all sorts of ways I was being shown that and told it in and through family and friends. I don't think that my parents, my family and my friends would be comfortable with the title of "disciples", "witnesses" to the Kingdom, but that is what they were and are in so many ways.

Yes, it is a challenging task, a daunting mission, for those of us in priestly ministry and, indeed, for all God's People; but many have been doing it and haven't realised. So we must keep on asking the Lord of the harvest, we must keep on encouraging labourers to go out and work; we must carry on with our mission like lambs among wolves and remember to preach by our lives that the Kingdom of God is very near.

We are on this pilgrimage together. We are not on our own no matter who we are, and it hasn't finished yet. We need one another on the journey of discerning and living out our vocations. I certainly need help, support and encouragement now and into the future and, I suspect, so do you. So let's allow St Augustine to have the last encouraging words.

"Let us sing 'Alleluia' here below while we are still anxious so that we may sing it one day there above when we are freed from care. How happy will be our shout of 'Alleluia' there, how carefree, how secure from any adversary, where there is no enemy where no friend perishes… Here praise is offered to God by people who are anxious, it is offered in hope, it is offered there by people who are enjoying the reality; here it is offered by people who are pilgrims, there by people who have reached their own country. So brethren, now let us sing 'Alleluia'… Sing as travellers, sing along the road, but keep on walking … go forward in virtue, in true faith and right conduct. Sing up and keep on walking."

(St Augustine, sermon 256,3)

Alleluia. Amen

Bishop Terence Drainey, Bishop of Middlesbrough.

Flowing Waters

Fr John Farrell OP

The prophet Ezekiel writes of his vision of a new Temple. From its threshold flows living water which brings to the desert life, fruitfulness and health (Ezek 47). It is an image of the ecology of grace flowing from the wounded side of Christ.

The Catholic pastoral priest lives on the banks of this river and is called to be a poet of the varied landscapes of salvation at work. He knows that the kingdom has not yet come "on earth as it is in heaven". He experiences daily the fragility of goodness, the complexities of love and love gone wrong and the downright nastiness of which human beings are capable. Yet he also knows that divine grace flows through human life and through our human landscapes.

We are today fascinated by ecology and the diversity and richness of life on our planet. As Aquinas says, if the natural world is so diverse, how much more so is the supernatural (Ia.q.50a.3). The Holy Spirit does not flow through the Trinity's good creation without bearing fruit. The pastoral priest is called to be an ecologist of the Trinity-in-action: "'My Father continues working and so do I' says the Lord" (Jn 5:17).

At times a priest can be overwhelmed by the collapse of communities, the loneliness of poverty and the helplessness of society's underdogs. He can feel left behind by the flow of his own culture's rush into secularism. But consecrated by Christ to the service of others, he is in touch with the greater rhythm and force of divine providence. It is of this he is to speak and even to sing, whether it be in praise or lamentation.

Let us take one common feature of contemporary parish life: the breakdown of marriage and other relationships. Many of our parishioners are left alone, broken-hearted, betrayed, burdened with financial anxieties and with the care of their children when marriages or long term relationships fail. The pastor "whose eyes are opened" may often see here an unexpected flowering of graces hidden from the certain and the devout. When Thomas Aquinas is redefining the macho, militaristic Greek virtue of Courage he sees it in its Christian context as "sticking at what is right despite the difficulties" and it is not a short term matter but one of "perseverance over time". Our fellow parishioners have often to continue to look after themselves, their children, their homes and jobs even though their world has collapsed around them, their self-worth has been destroyed and even their memories have been betrayed as false. Here we see Courage in the lives of ordinary women and men in their on-going commitment to their families, their responsibilities, their own sense of self-worth – an endurance that can be costly and lonely.

We priests know in ourselves that long-term endurance brings with it the danger of a hardening of heart and a dulling of involvement, but to our surprise and joy we often find among our own parishioners what Aquinas calls the third part of Courage – magnanimity – a largeness of heart. It is often the most broken-hearted who are the largest-hearted, the most expansive in self-giving, in time and welcome. Aquinas's fourth and last part of Courage is "magnificence". In its Greek origin this relates to militaristic glory and shining armour. In its Christian setting it is the gleam of deep-down earthly goodness, of divine grace in human lives and the shimmer of the kingdom at work among us – the presence of "heaven in ordinarie".

When the pastor gives the body and blood of Christ to his people he rarely knows the pathways of providence they are treading at the crossroad of that Holy Communion, or the anxieties they bring with them. In the sacrifice of the Mass they and he together offer their petitions and thanks within the all-powerful prayer of Christ the High Priest in his once and for all sacrifice. The pastoral priest will know that he is surrounded by holiness far greater than his own. He knows too he is also in an environment of foolishness, spite, envy and sometimes downright malice. This is the world which God so loved that he gave up his Son. These are the people for whom Christ died.

In the ancient truth that comes from the Apostles, in the rituals of the traditions, in the Sacred Word and the Holy Sacraments and in the lived life of the People he stands beside the flowing waters.

Fr John Farrell OP, Prior Provincial of the Dominican Order.

Part-time Priest?

Archbishop Michael Fitzgerald M Afr.

It is now forty-eight years since Cardinal Godfrey ordained me to serve the Missionaries of Africa (The White Fathers). There followed seven years of further studies, in theology and in Arabic and Islamic studies. The next ten years were spent in academic work – Arabic, Islam and Philosophy in Rome and in Uganda. This was followed by two years in a parish in a small town near the Ethiopian border ministering to a small Christian community in a largely Muslim area. I expected to return to academic work in Rome, but instead I was elected to the General Council of the Society of Missionaries of Africa and later found myself appointed to the Secretariat for Non Christians – later to become the Pontifical Council for Interreligious Dialogue. Eventually, in February 2006, Pope Benedict appointed me Apostolic Nuncio in Cairo and Delegate to the League of Arab States.

What has the priesthood meant to me during these years? There have been times of doubt, times when I have wondered whether it was really necessary to be a priest to teach Arabic or to foster interreligious relations. Strangely enough, questions of an opposite nature arose during the time in Sudan. Many of the people in the area our parish served were so poor that I felt I would have been able to help them more if I had been a qualified nurse or social worker.

I have been reassured by a passage from *The Attitude of the Church toward the Followers of Other Religions* (Secretariat for Non Christians, 1984). It states that the mission of the Church is "a single but complex and articulated reality". It indicates its principal elements: the "simple presence" of a Christian community; "commitment to the service of mankind and all forms of activity for social development"; "liturgical life and that of prayer and contemplation"; "the dialogue in which Christians meet the followers of other religious traditions"; "announcement and catechesis in which the good news of the Gospel is proclaimed and its consequences for life and culture are analysed" (N.13).

All of these activities belong to the mission of the Church and they have to be carried forward together. Can there not be particular vocations for these different aspects? There are some priests who are called to be pastors, some called to the contemplative life, some to social action, some to preaching and catechesis. So why should some priests not discover that their particular vocation lies in reaching out to people who are not Christians, helping to build with them relations of harmony and peace? What is important is that none of the elements listed should be seen as exclusive of the others. They are to be carried out in the spirit of unity, accepting that members of the Body of Christ play different roles, but always at the service of the one Church.

In Uganda I was in the strange position of being a Catholic priest lecturing about Islam to, among others, Muslim students. I am sure that the fact of being known as a priest, sometimes engaged in the Catholic chaplaincy at the university, was actually an asset. It witnessed to a religious spirit, and thus reinforced the respect I tried to show for Muslims and for Islam, following the teaching of Vatican II's *Nostra Aetate*.

Nor did the fact of being priest, or bishop, hinder relations with Buddhists or Hindus, Muslims, Sikhs or Zoroastrians. That priests would dedicate themselves to this activity was a sign that the Church was attentive to people belonging to other religious traditions. At the same time there was ample opportunity to witness to the Catholic faith in a gentle and courteous manner. For the priest himself, it is important that the people who are met in this way, in different parts of the world, become subjects of the conversation with God in prayer, and are brought before Him during the Eucharist.

I must admit, however, that I probably would have had difficulty in living the priesthood in this way if I had not had some pastoral activity: celebrating the Eucharist and the sacrament of reconciliation; being invited to administer confirmation and giving retreats. I am grateful to the people who have had recourse to my ministry, stimulating me to reflect and pray on Scripture, helping me to achieve a certain unity in my life as a priest. In fact, with the help of God's grace, in all the different missions entrusted to me, I have lived fully as a priest, and not just as a part-time priest.

Archbishop Michael Fitzgerald M Afr., Apostolic Nuncio to Egypt.

Enjoy the Life the Lord Has Given

Canon Reginald Fuller

Canon Reginald Cuthbert Fuller, better known as "Reggie" was born on 12 September 1908 and at the age of 100 is the oldest priest in the Archdiocese of Westminster. He was ordained in 1931 by Cardinal Francis Bourne which means that he will celebrate his 78th anniversary of Ordination this year. He lives in retirement at Nazareth House, Finchley where he is very well looked after and concelebrates Mass most days. When one visits him it is evident that his fine mind is remarkably alert and he is very well able to hold court on whatever subject he wishes to expound upon.

The son of the physician and medical author, Arthur William Fuller, he was born in London and brought up in St Johns Wood where his father practiced medicine. Initially he was sent to Ealing Priory School where he was to forge a life long friendship with John Bernard Orchard who subsequently became a monk of Ealing Abbey; they were both destined to make considerable advances in the study of Scripture. Reggie was a co-founder of the Catholic Biblical Association of Great Britain and a member of the Revised Standard Version Bible Committee and a Co-Editor of the first complete Bible translation in modern English for Catholics from the Hebrew and the Greek.

After Ealing he then went to Ampleforth College where he recalls with pleasure his involvement in the sporting life of the college, particularly rugby and cross country running. From there he went to Allen Hall Seminary, St Edmund's College, Ware for five years. After Ordination in Westminster Cathedral he was sent to Rome to continue his academic studies where he gained a doctorate in sacred theology from the Angelicum University, a licence in scripture from the Biblical Institute and much later in life in the early 1960s he took up biblical research at Cambridge University where he earned his Ph.D.

All of this brings to mind the story of the rather grand lady who is reputed to have gone to him for confession when he was the parish priest of Our Lady of the Assumption and St Gregory, Warwick Street and who asked him if he was a Jesuit. When he replied that he was not, but rather a diocesan priest, she replied: "Oh what a pity, I suppose some of you have to be in the ranks!"

Not surprisingly he was destined to lecture in Biblical Studies at Allen Hall, then at the teachers training college at St Mary's, Strawberry Hill, and then spent three years at the University of Nairobi, in Kenya where he lectured in Old Testament studies. When one meets him it is clear that this was a much treasured period of his life. He got to know Africa really well and he told me that he has never really left Africa. There he indulged his passion as an intrepid mountain climber and came close on more than one occasion to losing his life.

When I asked him about his long life as a priest and what he would want to impart to his brethren he said that it "was difficult to enunciate principles now" but that it was important to get them right at the beginning of priestly life. If someone sets out to "achieve personal advancement – forget it!" He was adamant that "we should enjoy the life the Lord has given to us as priests." He felt that for the most part his nigh on seventy-eight years of priesthood were happy ones, sometimes boring, but most importantly he valued the friendships he had made.

No account of Reggie's life could omit the deep friendship he was privileged to have with Group Captain Lord Leonard Cheshire that great convert to the church whose powerful spirituality was evident to anyone who was lucky enough to meet him. His prayer life was so deep that when you were conscious of his presence at a Mass you were celebrating he made you celebrate with even greater devotion than was customary. Leonard Cheshire and his wife Sue Ryder were to achieve so much in their own life times and help so many people with the respective homes they set up; whatever part Reggie played in supporting and encouraging them must be part of his own legacy too.

Canon Reginald Fuller has the distinction of being the only Honorary Canon in the Diocese of Westminster, which is the result of a spontaneous act of kindness on the part of Cardinal Cormac Murphy-O'Connor, who decided he wanted to honour Reggie on the occasion of his 70th anniversary of Ordination in 2001. Quite what may happen in two years time when he looks well set to celebrate his 80th we shall wait to see. *Ad multos annos* Reggie from all of us.

Compiled by Canon Daniel Cronin.

Canon Reginald Fuller is a retired priest of the Archdiocese of Westminster.

Pastoral Charity and Virtues

Francis Cardinal George OMI

People come to priests not because they are sinless – if ever anybody imagined that to be the case, they know differently now. People will continue to come to priests because they know they must gather around them if they are to be visibly one in Christ. The ordained priesthood is where Christ's authority for the salvation of his people is exercised and made visible. But it is authority given to them to give life to others: God's own life for the salvation of the world. Priests are life-givers. That means that a priest's life must be one of integrity. The integrity of any Christian life is protected by virtues, which are habits of life that enable us, without a constant struggle, to live faithfully with the grace that Christ wants to give us here so that we may have its fulfilment in the life to come.

Since the Second Vatican Council, we've spoken about the primary virtue of ordained priests as pastoral charity. Before that, the primary virtue of priests was usually described as zeal. A good priest is a zealous priest, zealous for the salvation of the world. I think, however, that the reinterpretation of zeal as pastoral charity is an advance in understanding what habits we need to live our life with integrity. For pastoral charity says not just zeal for the salvation of the world but love for the world. No one can evangelise someone he doesn't love. You cannot speak of evangelising a culture unless you are able to participate in it and show that you love it. A zealot is not an evangeliser. Only someone whose life is marked by love has the ability to reveal the Father's self-giving in generative love for the world. In pastoral charity love is not general but ascetic, in a particular manner. One who is pastoral is sacrificing himself for the people. The type of availability to the people that is intrinsic, that is integral, to priestly ministry is a form of spiritual ascesis, a form of penance, of self-discipline. Pastoral charity is a self-sacrificing love. That is the primary virtue that is to inform the life of priests, but it has to be protected by other priestly virtues that see to it that pastoral charity is always vital so that we can persevere as life givers. Three of these virtues are faith, a priest's surrender of his mind to Christ; obedience, a priest's surrender of his will to Christ; and chastity, a priest's surrender of his body to Christ for love of his people. These virtues protect the practice of pastoral charity and are necessary for its integrity.

Francis Cardinal George OMI, Archbishop of Chicago.

Military Chaplaincy

Fr Nick Gosnell

On the second day of serving as a chaplain in the Army I was tasked with conducting the weekly Church Parade for the Irish Guards. Mindful of the need to engage one's audience as soon as possible, I posed what I took to be a rhetorical question: "So, what would've happened if Jesus hadn't been born?" I asked, prior to my intention to go on to draw out the lessons of the incarnation in a world of violence and war. Unfortunately, the average infantryman doesn't always grab the niceties of grammatical nuance and before I could proceed a voice from the back shouted: "Well, you'd be out of a ruddy job for a start!" It was a crash course in squaddie humour and a salutary lesson in how "what you see is what you get in the world" into which I had been propelled.

As a married man I was sent by my Bishop (Cardinal Basil Hume, OSB) into the Forces soon after ordination for, by his own admission, purely pragmatic reasons. First, I had served as a nurse in the Royal Navy prior to training as an Anglican priest and so had some previous military experience and second, at that time the Catholic Church was still coming to terms about the practicalities of supporting a priest who came with the responsibilities of a wife and two young children. In letting the Ministry of Defence pay and house and employ me I could exercise my priesthood in a worthwhile environment whilst not being a burden on the finances of the diocese. Benedictines have always had an uncanny grasp of the way the world really works!

The challenges and opportunities are a constant surprise and revelation when serving God in his people in various places around the globe. This could be battling against the natural elements and the hatred of neighbours because of their ethnicity in Kosovo, or acting as a neutral assessor in the selection process of potential Ghurkha soldiers in Nepal and conducting Remembrance Day services for the Ambassador and ex-pat community in Kathmandu. It might be training with Paras in Kuwait before heading north as chaplain with a Close Support Medical Regiment in Iraq during the war phase, or chatting with men and women repairing tanks on a vehicle park on Salisbury Plain, or engaging with a recruit who has just joined the Army and is feeling homesick. It might be conducting interviews with all sorts and shapes and hues of soldiers about anything from sexual harassment to marriage preparation, to fear of going to sleep and reliving the night they were involved in a fire-fight that killed their best friend. In these varied ways there is always a chance to witness to the compassion of the Risen Lord, even if the one for whom the energy and concentration is expended has either lapsed from their faith or never had one in the first place.

None of this would be possible, and at best most of it would be a poor imitation of social care, if it were not for the fact that the minister of grace in such circumstances is rooted in the prayer of the Church and nourished by the exercise of a ministry of sacramental truth. Celebrating the gifts of God with the people of God sustains and encourages all priests in their calling, not least when they find themselves so constantly in alien environments, both physically and spiritually. Without this we are merely frail human vessels, but with it we are warriors for Christ.

What we do, and how we do it, often defies description and maybe that's just as well. During a recent deployment when the rockets and mortars were raining down upon our position indiscriminately every day, and wearing full body armour wherever you went (including the shower!) in 50 degrees of heat, I dived into a shallow depression upon hearing the air-raid indicate that more death and destruction was heading our way. A second later a rather large corporal from the catering platoon fell in on top of me in order to gain some protection for himself. "Ah, it's you Father," he said as he recognised me in the confusion of the moment. "You know," he continued as we awaited our fate, "I've been meaning to say for a while that I don't know what it is that you do, but I'm ruddy glad that you're here doing it." "Thanks for that," I replied, still catching my breath, "but the pleasure's all mine. After all, if something does go wrong, I've got you on top of me as an extra layer of protection!" The ministry of incarnation; thank God for it!

Fr Nick Gosnell, CF(RC), Chaplain, 1st Regiment, Royal Horse Artillery.

The Hiddenness of Priestly Life

Fr James Hanvey SJ

When things are in transition and the old certainties, languages and systems seem to be dissolving, the question of identity becomes a recurring anxiety. Although the sacrament of priesthood confers its own immutable character, identity is always worked out in a context, in a community, in relationships. As these change then so will the experience of ministry and its range. In this situation identity will appear unstable and meaning difficult to establish with confidence. Yet, in an odd way the immutable character of the sacrament of priesthood commits the priest to these relationships in all their fluidity – relationships he does not choose but is given; relationships that he cannot simply shake off.

Even when such relationships are at their most painful, somehow they continue to shape and determine a life, a ministry, a way of being. The sacrament does not remove the priest from the world, from the lives of the people he is called to serve, from the Church that walks the rough path of history, living with generosity and love in cultures that are hostile or simply uncomprehending. Instead it commits him more completely and more insistently to live in all these realities. Always in his life is the dynamic of the incarnation. It carries him beyond himself into the depths of the world, the secret places of the human heart and the human dream and, of course, the brokenness of both.

He lives there, with his people, knowing the poverty of his own resources; the daily encounter with his fragility and the many things he does not know, the answers he does not have. In these moments he can only trust to the future – not so much a time but a person whom he has come to know and live as his Lord. He lives with the struggle, with the pull to withdraw – just a little – to take control and to measure out his energy, choose his paths and find his resting places. He knows that he was not called for his strengths but for his weakness. He knows that those consoling words of Paul, that God's strength is perfected in his weakness, are not empty words. But when he has to drink from the cup of weakness or eat the bread of his loneliness, when the drag of routine can almost hollow out any strong sense of identity that has life, it is not easy to live these things as a real grace, a real moment of meeting with the God who has called him. But if he does not give in to fear, rush into activity or find some theology or spirituality that will offer comfort and security, if he can hand himself over to the faith the Church has in him and remain faithful to the sacrament at the centre of his life, something begins to disclose itself. Slowly, over a lifetime, he does not discover an answer but an act, a way of being. It is a way of being hidden.

Our culture makes us want to know who we are. It commands us to "be ourselves", to be the masters and the makers of our lives; this is the ultimate freedom. But the priest is not self-made; all he has, he has received. This is the mystery at the centre of his life and in every moment he is "given", "handed over". He remains an enigma to himself, a puzzle, because he can never be in command of the sacrament that has now claimed him; the One who has made his home in him. All he can do is receive himself from the sacrament which is effective in every minute of his life whatever his situation or condition.

As a priest, his life moves in the very opposite direction of "sovereign self". In the very moment of receiving himself he can only let go, let himself be given. Given in all those small and unnoticed ways; in the ordinariness of sacraments which he celebrates for God's people, in the prayers he says, sometimes badly and distractedly; in all the lives he touches, sometimes absentmindedly, sometimes with love and insight and care; and in those hidden moments when someone opens their life to him in its pain and despair, its guilt and its shame, when somehow he finds a word or maybe no word, but his presence is an unacknowledged healing. So, in this daily rhythm of receiving and being given he allows himself to be shaped by the ebb and flow of grace, alive in the rhythm of the Spirit breathing in him. He allows himself to be lost in the life of the Church. He gives himself to the unsung gestures of love and he recognises that on some days, just some days, he might understand a little of their beauty and their mystery.

Occasionally, if he's attentive and faithful to the rhythms of this sacrament that has become his life, he might begin to glimpse a form, another life that moves within his own without which he would have no life. He might recognise the One in whose life his own lies immersed and hidden. And when he comes each day to say those simple words, not his own words but the words he has been given, he knows he is in the school of love. "Take and receive…" Not just words but an act; an act which he knows he can never fathom or exhaust. Here, pronounced and performed, he is born to himself and to Christ and to his people. He will know the Life he carries; the joy, even in sacrifice and surrender, of being poured out and given away. In these words which he is given to speak, his life has become a Eucharist; a "yes" which he says yet knows is always beyond him. "Take and receive." Here, in this act, all the hidden surrenders gather into Love, into Christ, and he knows whose identity he carries. He knows himself in living this Life beyond his own.

Take Lord, and receive
All my liberty, my memory, my understanding,
    and my entire will,
All I have and possess. You have given all to me.

To you, Lord, I return it.
All is yours, dispose of it wholly according
     to your will.
Give me your love and your grace, for this is
     sufficient for me.

(St Ignatius of Loyola. Sp. Exx. 234)

Fr James Hanvey SJ is Superior of the Jesuit Community at Farm Street, London and Director of Research, the Heythrop Institute for Religion, Ethics and Public Life, Heythrop College, London.

Priesthood – An Experience and Communication of Love

Archbishop Denis Hart

As a teenager I was conscious of being loved by God. The Jesuit priests who were in the parish and school which I attended were all different personalities. All were united by a search for personal holiness and a commitment to draw people into a personal relationship with Christ, the great High Priest. Prayer as personal friendship with Jesus was always emphasised.

Young people are blessed with very high ideals, but often doubt their ability to live up to them. When a young man offers himself for priesthood in answer to God's loving call he enters into a mysterious journey, which engages his heart, mind and will. It reassures him and challenges him in the years of seminary formation. Deep and lasting friendships are established in that time, which become a lifetime support.

As the seminary years pass there is an increasing desire for ordination. We long to be a priest of worship and to engage with the daily lives of people, helping them to experience how God loves and treasures them.

At the invitation of God the Father, Jesus became the great High Priest when he came on earth, lived and died and rose again.

On the day of Ordination the Church calls a man to be another Christ.

Priestly life is tremendously varied and engaging. Daily Mass, the Liturgy of the Hours and time of prayer deepens the friendship with the Lord. In celebrating Mass and the Sacraments the priest stands as a bridge to draw people to God and to show God's love to the men, women and children of today. This personal contact is extended in visits to people in their homes, schools, in community and parish groups, where a deep relationship of support and love is forged between people and priest. In these visits the priest is a visible sign of the love of God which we personally experience at the altar.

People welcome their priests as the human face illustrating God's nearness to them as they grapple with the many pressures of modern living. God is near and through us he loves them.

I have always been humbled at the trust placed in priests and by the invitation which people give us into profound aspects of their lives. This further illustrates how they long for God. This pastoral engagement in people's daily lives makes us grow into greater nearness with him.

We priests have unique gifts to offer in parish, school and hospital. Other areas of administration, social work and teaching are further extensions of our care because priests are chosen to be "all things to all men that we might save some". Other requests will come from the community, various work places, the Parliament, the prisons. Here again our priestly gifts are needed.

All of these possibilities illustrate the universal hunger of people for authentic love. Many priests whom I admire speak of the vocation of a diocesan priest as intertwined with the lives of their people, sharing their joys and sufferings.

Celibate love is a personal relationship with the Lord. We can trust him unfailingly as our hearts are made large to love our people in the same way and with the same effect as Jesus did.

Priests are loved and supported by the people. In every parish and community I visit I find a love of the priesthood, a desire to give and receive support and a tremendous longing to know Jesus more deeply in their lives. Our vocation is to entrust ourselves to the Lord knowing his support that through our prayer, words and deeds Jesus will walk the homes and streets of our parishes and cities.

Archbishop Denis Hart, Archbishop of Melbourne.

Priesthood: Living the Tradition

Fr Michael Hayes

In June 2008 I felt drawn to visit St Isidore's College in Rome. It had been the Irish Franciscan College and its church is situated off a side street. The College was closed when I visited it but a caretaker did eventually let me in. I was there because that was where my grand-uncle, Fr Aidan Roberts OFM, had been ordained a Franciscan priest a hundred years before, on 13 June 1908. Although I never knew the man, and indeed very little about his life as a priest, I did feel an extraordinary connection. The familial connection made him part of my blood family, but the priestly connection was very significant, even though I knew nothing of what sort of a ministry he had exercised or how effective he was as a priest. I stood in the sanctuary and found myself giving thanks for the life and ministry of someone I never knew but felt very connected to.

It is now nearly thirty years since my own ordination, and during that time, I have read a great deal about the ministerial priesthood, and spent long hours on retreat and in priestly ministry groups reflecting on "priesthood". I can honestly say that I now feel I know less about what ordination means than ever before – that is mainly because the richness of the experience of years makes neat definitions seem flippant. At the same time I can, however, say I feel far more comfortable in ministry because that experience with its strains and its joys, has given me a deeper appreciation of being a priest.

I can sit more comfortably in priesthood now, because the Letter to the Hebrews has in recent years given me both insight and assurance on the meaning of priesthood. Priesthood can never be mine, rather it is a gift that I am privileged to share in. It is a sharing in the Priesthood of Christ the High Priest. Sharing in the privilege of that calling, but also in the consequences of that calling: "During his life on earth, he offered up prayer and entreaty, aloud and in silent tears, to the one who had the power to save him out of death, and he submitted so humbly that his prayer was heard" (Heb 5:7).

I have lived most of my ministerial life not in a parish setting but in the context of academic life. This means that at times my work seems very "unpriestly" in certain obvious ways – though I have no doubt about the truly priestly nature of being present in the world which Christ sanctifies through the work of all the people of God. But I have come to appreciate the truth that as those who share in the priesthood of Christ – lay and ordained – our gathering for liturgy is the source and summit of our Christian living. I cherish more and more the small praying community that I celebrate the Eucharist with each Sunday. It is this experience on a weekly basis above all that nourishes and sustains me.

For me these four short paragraphs summarise the priesthood which has passed down from generation to generation to serve the people of God; the experience of ministry nourishes and validates my calling; that calling makes any sense only in relationship to Christ's priesthood; and it is lived out in prayer with the worshipping community.

Fr Michael Hayes is a priest of the Archdiocese of Southwark, a Vice-Principal at St Mary's University College, Twickenham, Middlesex and editor of *The Pastoral Review*.

Priesthood – A Monastic View

Fr Andrew Henson OCSO

The Decree of the Second Vatican Council on the Ministry and Life of Priests puts great emphasis on the apostolic missionary activity of priests in building up the Church. So is there a place for the exercise of the Priesthood in a contemplative community? Yes, for "The Eucharist is … the beginning and end of all preaching of the Gospel." *(Presbyterorum Ordinis 4)* and "No Christian community can be built without roots and foundations in the celebration of the Most Holy Eucharist." (P.O.7) – and this must include also the contemplative community. The monk who is a priest presides in his turn at the Community Mass, he administers the other sacraments to members of the Community, to the guests, and to those who live in the ambience of the monastery, and shares with them the understanding and wisdom that he has acquired. Although his external ministry is confined within the limits of the monastery and its environs, like St Paul he experiences "anxiety for all the churches." (2 Cor 11:28), and indeed for all the world. Sometimes he will feel a personal helplessness in the face of conflicts, disasters, injustice; but he believes that the ardent prayer of a heart united to Christ is more efficacious to overcome evil than any amount of activity without devotion.

St Benedict has a terse precept for a monk who is ordained priest: "Let him advance more and more in godliness." The disposition of radical consecration to the love of Christ and the service of the Church which is characteristic of the monastic vocation accords perfectly with the configuration to Christ the Good Shepherd, which is the ideal of the Priesthood. The ministry of the monk-priest is an adventure of total love and dedication. The embers of sacrificial charity which glow brightly in his heart spring readily into lively flames under the breath of the Holy Spirit, whenever he is called upon to celebrate Mass, to provide the Sacrament of Reconciliation, or perhaps to give advice and encouragement to his brethren in the Diocesan Priesthood. As the "Friend of the Bridegroom" he forgets his own convenience and integrates his ministry into this monastic routine. Despite his awareness that he is an unworthy servant, an "urchin priest", he knows that he is held close to the bosom of Christ like the Beloved Disciple, and that Mary, the Mother of all priests, watches over him.

The closing off of earthly ambition, the exclusion of major distractions which might lead him to deviate from the real purpose of the monastic and priestly vocation, leave room for the Holy Spirit to lead him forward in single-minded devotion to an ever deeper love of Jesus. The monastic way of life leads to purity of heart, and the time comes when the monk-priest can fully understand that "God saw everything that he had made, and it was very good" (Gen 1:31). So he can embrace with an undivided heart all who come into his life and enter into deep and enriching friendships. Life becomes a continuous Advent, in which the prayer of the early Church "Come, Lord Jesus" takes on more urgency. Fidelity during many years brings the expectation of a joy beyond all telling, in communion with the Lord Jesus, with parents and friends and with all who have persevered in the hope of attaining God's Kingdom.

Fr Andrew Henson OCSO, a Cistercian Monk of Mount Saint Bernard Abbey in Leicestershire.

Tired?

Fr Stefan Hnylycia

As the battle for Helm's Deep approaches in Tolkien's *The Lord of the Rings*, Gimli the dwarf exclaims: "Sleep! I feel the need of it, as never I thought any dwarf could… Yet my axe is restless in my hand. Give me a row of orc-necks and room to swing and all weariness will fall from me!"

We all know about being tired. It is something real and part of our human condition. Jesus once took the Apostles away to get some rest, though on that occasion things worked out differently. It is important to look after our rest and that of our brother priests prudently but with the mind that Christ Jesus showed.

As with other areas of life, one needs to avoid extremes. I once met a priest who felt he could never take a day off from his parish; he felt bound to stay put day after day. At the other end of the scale are the parishioners who might read in the parish newsletter how "Father would be away", yet again, "taking a well earned rest".

The Gospel gives us insights into how to see and balance things more supernaturally.

St Mark tells us of a Sabbath day our Lord spent in Capernaum. In the synagogue Jesus preached to everyone's amazement. Then there was a challenging moment of the man with an unclean spirit. On leaving the synagogue Jesus went to the house of Simon Peter to eat and recover his strength. But what did he find there? "Now Simon's mother-in-law lay sick with a fever, and immediately they told him of her. And he came and took her by the hand and lifted her up, and the fever left her."

After dinner and as it turned dark, there was a knock at the door. Who hasn't shared this experience: a knock at the presbytery door or phone call on a Sunday evening? Just when I was going to put my feet up, or check my email, or even spend some time with brother priests?

We know well Christ's response to that crowd who came looking for healing from the Good Shepherd and Divine Physician of souls. And so, our Blessed Lord works on into the night for who knows how long? Scripture goes on to relate that on the following morning Jesus rose very early and went out to pray. No doubt he was tired, as were those in Simon Peter's household.

Our Lord's response ought to make us think. He is moved to prayer; he tells his companions that they must be off to other places so that his work may continue.

Thankfully, our calling is not to hew "orc necks". Through our ordination we share in Christ's work as Good Shepherd and Divine Physician of souls. Ours is to "hew out" the damage done to Christ's flock through sin and ignorance: to bind wounds, to counsel, to encourage, to raise up.

Fatigue is a component of work, but it is precisely in doing our Lord's work that our hearts and minds are led to gratitude in prayer and greater apostolic zeal.

A priest who offered to help hearing confessions last Good Friday found himself there for two and a half hours. Tiring? Without doubt. He "emerged" content and joyous at having had that experience.

Let our hearts then be in the mould of the One who called us. Tiredness we will meet. Let it be though, Lord, your tiredness when tending your flock. And let us be vigilant for one another so that tiredness does not lead to unnecessary exhaustion.

Fr Stefan Hnylycia is a priest of the Opus Dei Prelature. He lives and works in London.

The Contradiction of the Cross

Bishop Alan Hopes

The opening antiphon of the Holy Thursday Mass is: *We should glory in the Cross of Christ.* It is a curious statement and yet we make it boldly and gladly. For the Sacrifice of the Cross, instituted tonight, offered tomorrow and effected on Easter Sunday, is our assurance of God's redeeming love which will never fail. The Cross is indeed a sign of contradiction – for though the Cross is at the heart of our faith, we proclaim through the Cross our belief in *life*. Others might proclaim their belief in death – we consistently affirm that we believe in life.

A great deal is being asked of those who are called to the ministerial priesthood of the Church. It is a noble vocation. It is a joyous vocation. It is also a vocation of sacrifice. That which we do, that we also live. I believe that there is a deep offering of hope to the world in a vocation which expects a way of life so much in contradiction to that which is accepted as "normal" in everyday life.

The great driving forces of money, sex and power are the key motivators to most human endeavours. Without at least one of them, things seem to be pointless – there is no meaning to life. And yet the priest is expected to live simply and to give up the chance of amassing a great fortune. The priest is called to celibacy and to lay down that deep and personal side to our lives, the desire to be united intimately with another human being. The priest is called upon to renounce all worldly power and to be instead, someone who is obedient, someone who serves.

These are all signs of contradiction. They are signs of the Cross, which is the sign of contradiction and at the same time the sign of hope. Life makes sense. In being asked to live these particular evangelical counsels of poverty, chastity and obedience, we are being asked to be these signs of hope to a world where only success seems to matter.

This does not make us any better than our brothers and sisters in Christ, and it certainly does not remove any of those driving forces from us. But in hope, we embrace these values, uniting our offering with that of Christ on Calvary as we celebrate the Mass.

Bishop Alan Hopes, Auxiliary Bishop of Westminster.

Extract from the Holy Thursday homily preached to the students of the Royal College of St Alban, Vallodolid and the seminarians of the English College, Rome in Vallodolid, Holy Week 2008.

Ministering to the Needs of Others

Canon David Hopgood

In a geography lesson St Thérèse of Lisieux must have been asked to draw a map of England and Wales, for recently I was sent a copy of this school exercise that she undertook. I was delighted to see that among the few cities that she had highlighted was Portsmouth. Little did she know that she would be visiting this great port in September 2009 as her relics are to be welcomed into the Cathedral at Portsmouth. We never know what lies before us in our ministry and calling.

When we, as ordinands, place our hands in those of our ordaining Bishop, we promise respect and obedience. We do not promise to agree with everything the Bishop says or does – rather we commit ourselves to cooperate, collaborate and trust in the Bishop who can enable us to use our talents where he considers best for the Church we are called to serve.

My first two years of priestly life were eye opening and a steep learning curve. The parish, school and my parish priest taught me much of the skill of "priest-craft". The priesthood is about being open to the needs of the community, and not going in knowing all the answers. These were happy years, so when the Bishop asked me to leave and become his secretary I was devastated – I was not ordained to be an office bound priest in Portsmouth. I realised I had much to learn. The following seven years with the Bishop taught me an important lesson, that priesthood was about enabling. So when I, as secretary, enabled the Bishop to function I was being truly pastoral and fulfilling the priesthood that had been entrusted to me. The priesthood is about enabling and not necessarily about doing. This is surely collaboration.

After my time as the Bishop's secretary, to return

to parish life was a joy and welcome change, even though I know I made many mistakes as a parish priest. It was much more my intention not to go in with all the answers – rather to be with the community and listen to the needs and enable the ministry of others to flourish and grow. There is something about the priesthood that ensures that we never stop learning – perhaps because it is Christ's ministry that we are called to share in – in which case we will never stop learning how best to minister within the different circumstances in which we find ourselves.

I never thought that I would return to Portsmouth. When the Bishop asked me to come to the Cathedral, I was again tested in my promise of obedience, for being at the cathedral was not top of my list. Having said that, eleven years later I am pleased to have been a part of the restoration of this great building and, more importantly, to be a part of a community which has taught me the importance of the gift of hospitality.

Cathedrals are strange places. We have a strong parish community here but, like all other cathedrals, we also have a large group of transient people who seek anonymity, or have been hurt in other situations or communities and seek a refuge that asks nothing, but gives everything. To be a part of a community that listens and welcomes, regardless of situations, has confirmed in me yet another aspect of priestly ministry that we are called to – hospitality.

So it will be with a sense of privilege that we welcome yet another great visitor to the cathedral when we receive the relics of St Thérèse to Portsmouth Cathedral. I am sure that her great journey will bring many others on pilgrimage, enabling us to offer hospitality and the opportunity to listen and minister to them. Like this great saint, we really do not know where life will take us in the Lord's ministry. Perhaps for that we should thank God.

Canon David Hopgood, Dean of Portsmouth Cathedral.

Genuine Signs of Christ's Presence

Basil Cardinal Hume, OSB, OM

I would like you all to pray for me – and as time passes I see increasingly the urgency of that request – and I also pray that I may be "a genuine sign of Christ's loving presence among you". That applies to each of you as well. You are to be "a genuine sign of Christ's loving presence" among those entrusted to your pastoral care. As "genuine" signs of that presence, we must ourselves, as St Paul says, "put on Christ", that is to think as Christ thought, to act as Christ acted, to speak as Christ spoke. It is our task to ensure that the word of God is solemnly and properly acclaimed and the Catholic faith is taught, to make certain that the Eucharist and other liturgical services are celebrated with sincere devotion – and all this for the glory of God and for the well-being of the people we have been sent to serve. This last phrase could sound as if our laity were not more than the passive recipients of what we, as priests, have to offer. What an error that would be.

Just as the laity are expected now to play an active part in the liturgy – and this in consequence of their baptism – so must they also play an active part in the mission of the Church. It is part of our responsibility to work for the Kingdom of God in whatever way is most suitable and to enable the spiritual energies of the baptised to be released. It is for us to encourage them to learn more about their faith, to teach them how to pray, and to provide them with whatever assistance they may need to be missionaries, evangelisers and catechists in the circumstances of their daily lives.

Do not forget, too, that our lay people have been anointed with the Holy Spirit. He is at work in them as he is in us, and our leadership as priests – for bishops and priests must be leaders – will take account of this.

Ours, priest and people, is a partnership. We have different roles, but one purpose which is to give glory to God and to serve our neighbour – it is an adventure of love.

Basil Cardinal Hume OSB, OM. 1923 – 1999.
Abbot of Ampleforth 1963 – 1976 and Archbishop of Westminster 1976 – 1999.

An extract taken from *Light in the Lord,* St Paul Publications, 1991.

Ministry in a Secular Europe – The Case for a New Approach

Fr Paul Hypher

The coming decades in Europe will prove challenging. We are in the midst of a major historical shift in religious adherence, more significant than those shifts which followed the collapse of the Roman Empire, occurred during the Reformation, followed the age of Enlightenment and Revolution or which resulted from the Industrial Revolution.

Fewer than 20 percent of Europeans now regard religion as important (in the USA it is about 80 percent) and even fewer wish to offer religious values to their children. At no time has the Church been confronted with a society so devoid of religious sensitivity. We seem surprised at the speed of secularisation; yet we should have seen it coming.

Europe has more recently experienced four periods of mass alienation from religion – rural loss of contact in the eighteenth century; the unchurching of millions in the squalor and degradation of the cities of the Industrial Revolution; the slaughter of further millions of the working poor in the trenches of the first World War and now our present collapse.

During the first three, church structures were inappropriate for enabling the churches to be effective in remaining in solidarity alongside the victims of social change and war; worse still, many believed that the church itself was complicit in their misery. Methodism, the Evangelical Movement and, in the Catholic Church, the foundation of new apostolic religious orders tried to tackle the situation, but with limited success. There remained a huge effectively unchurched underclass.

This was the very group whose descendents

benefitted from the universal availability of Secondary and Tertiary education after World War II. By the 1960s, secularism ceased to be the prerogative of an intellectual elite, becoming instead the natural home of the now educated and often influential descendents of those marginalised by hardship and poverty over the previous two hundred years.

Solidarity is doing as Christ did – placing himself at one with the victims of oppression and deprivation. "It was essential that Christ should in this way become completely like his brothers so that he could be a compassionate and trustworthy high priest of God's religion, able to atone for human sins" (Heb 2:17). "Although he was Son, he learnt to obey through suffering; but having been made perfect, he became for all who obey him the source of eternal salvation" (Heb 5:8-9).

Jesus' solidarity with the worst of human predicaments is a constituent of His High Priesthood. (The other constituent is His being "made perfect" – his Resurrection.) Christ's solidarity is constituent of the Church as a Priestly People and also of Ministerial Priesthood. Indeed solidarity with the suffering and oppressed lies at the heart of the meaning of the Eucharist.

Our response to this crisis has been, however, to promote the in-gathering of the faithful to centralised places of pastoral ministry and worship. But this is to continue the previous approach, an approach which in fact prevented the Church from being a relevant presence in the lives of most people.

Suffering, poverty, deprivation, and oppression limit the scope of daily life – imprison rather than liberate, alienate rather than integrate, restrict rather than free.

Our priority must therefore be to restructure and diversify priesthood, ministry and our parish communities, making them apt for Christlike solidarity – face-to-face and flexible, closer to people (whether Catholic or not) where they are, working spiritually, liturgically and compassionately with those on the margins and alongside people in their places of deprivation and suffering.

This requires change in the formation of priests, a re-orientation of parishes, and smaller Eucharistic communities which are continually closer to those with whom Christ himself sought to be in solidarity.

Fr Paul Hypher is a retired priest of the Diocese of East Anglia.

We Share a Common Mystery

Fr Nicholas James

Thirty-two years have now passed since I arrived at my first parish and made my way towards the presbytery door. For two years I would be the assistant priest here, or "curate" as we were always called in those days. As I rang the doorbell of my new home and waited, I had no idea what to expect. The presbytery, hidden behind a jeweller's shop, was further concealed by its own secret garden; the church, a Georgian building, was large and faded. Both house and church were rather dusty windows on a vanished world.

My parish priest turned out to be a kindly teddy bear, whose Bobby Charlton hairstyle kept uncoiling and whose Canon's cassock seemed as ancient as the Georgian church he served. "We're strange creatures," he confided to me once. "We don't look normal in our ordinary clothes." A Kerry-man, he played the fiddle late at night and practised golf swings in the secret garden. Because he never drank, he never understood the etiquette of alcohol. Each visit of his friend, the Anglican cathedral Dean, would raise him to new heights of generosity; one man would offer, and the other in politeness struggle through, successive tumblers of whisky. His frequent diets were no less perplexing to me. Even when they kept him from potatoes, they always seemed to leave him free for ice-cream – a whole family block to himself.

We were opposites in every way but one; we shared a common mystery. We two were priests, ordained for all eternity, and that to him made all the difference. Nothing mattered more to him than that. Inside the church, a long unbroken altar rail marked out the sanctuary, and here, beneath two gloomy canvas paintings, a pair of ornate priedieux stood. This was our domain and this was where he felt we ought to pray, viewed sideways by the congregation, giving a good example to them all. I think I never found a setting less designed for unselfconscious prayer.

I sometimes wonder if that time was just a dream; and yet, beneath its fascinating strangeness I always recognised a deeper truth. He was a man who genuinely loved people; people he chanced to meet, people who arrived at the door seeking help; most of all he loved his own parishioners. I soon grew used to coming back from weekday Mass to find he'd gathered half the congregation at the breakfast table.

To me that was his first and greatest gift, though he may well have thought it lay elsewhere. He might have been much prouder of his grasp of metaphysics, his lifelong discipline of dress, or some arcane and sacerdotal quality only he and I could ever share.

In fact, for all the talk today about our lost transcendence and the way we ought to dress to make our role as priests quite clear, I often think of where I found transcendence then. It comes unbidden as a memory and leaves me with two lasting images of grace; of sunlight through the window on a room of laughing people and of waking every morning filled with joy.

Fr Nicholas James, Parish Priest of St Mary's, Monmouth.

A Priest!

Pope John Paul II

My ordination took place on an unusual day for such celebrations: it was on 1 November (1946), the Solemnity of All Saints, when the Church's liturgy is wholly directed to celebrating the mystery of the Communion of Saints and preparing to commemorate the faithful departed. The Archbishop had chosen that date because I was scheduled to leave for Rome to continue my studies. I was ordained by myself, in the private chapel of the Archbishop of Cracow. My classmates were to be ordained the following year, on Palm Sunday.

Veni, Creator Spiritus!

> I can still remember myself in that chapel during the singing of *Veni, Creator Spiritus* and the Litany of the Saints, lying prostrate on the floor with arms outstretched in the form of a cross, awaiting the moment of the imposition of hands. It was a very moving experience! Subsequently I have presided many times over this same rite as a Bishop and as Pope. There is something very impressive about the prostration of the ordinands, symbolising as it does their total submission before the majesty of God and their complete openness to the action of the Holy Spirit who will descend upon them and consecrate them.

Veni, Creator Spiritus, mentes Tuorum visita, imple superna gratia quae Tu creasti pectora.

> Just as in the Mass the Holy Spirit brings about the transubstantiation of the bread and wine

into the Body and Blood of Christ, so also in the Sacrament of Holy Orders he effects the priestly or episcopal consecration. The Bishop who confers the Sacrament of Holy Orders is the human dispenser of this divine mystery. The imposition of hands is the continuation of the gesture used by the early Church to signify that the Holy Spirit is being given for a specific mission (cf. Acts 6:6, 8:17, 13:3). Paul imposed hands on the disciple Timothy (cf. 2 Tim 1:6; 1 Tim 4:14), and the gesture has remained in the Church (cf. 1 Tim 5:22) as the efficacious sign of the Holy Spirit's active presence in the Sacrament of Holy Orders.

Pope John Paul II 1920-2005.

Extract from *Gift and Ministry*, Doubleday/Catholic Truth Society, 1997. © Libreria Editrice Vaticana 1996.

Christ in the Prison

Mgr Malachy Keegan

I joined the Prison Service as a chaplain, in 1998. I have spent most of my life, since then, in prisons. At first I was conscious of being in a strange and it seemed a threatening new world. Gradually, I began to feel, in a way, at home! "We knew you would end up in prison," some of my friends jokingly said. I began to feel a certain solidarity with all the people who live and work in our prisons.

I began to ask myself why it felt so right to be in places where pain and healing, despair and hope, live side by side.

I celebrate Mass in prison chapels for congregations of men, women and young people, for people who may only spend weeks in prison or for those who may spend the whole of their natural lives there. Sometimes, the congregation may be elderly, sometimes young, sometimes people from other parts of the world, sometimes people who are very fragile and vulnerable, sometimes people living with memories of awful crimes committed. Nonetheless, I noticed something remarkable in them all – an openness to the Lord's words, "Come to me, all you who labour and are burdened, and I will give you rest."

I began to think of the man executed on a cross next to the dying Jesus, who while acknowledging his sinfulness yet uttered those most moving words of Faith, "Remember me when you come into your Kingdom." The Lord's reply was unconditional, "Today you will be with me in Paradise." Yes, it was a convicted criminal who was the first person the Lord was able to bring safely home to Heaven!

What a privilege it is to be with someone who suddenly or gradually discovers a need for God. Moments of such Grace come frequently in prisons. Why? I discovered it was because the good Lord resides in our prisons and waits there for those moments of trust in the human heart which enable him to embrace us in love.

The great Welsh poet, R.S. Thomas recognised prison as a place where God dwells:

> "We ransack the heavens, the distance between stars;
> The last place we look in prison, his hideout in flesh
>   and bone."

"Flesh and bone" is usually the way the Lord appears. He comes clothed in flesh and bone. I have met so many priest prison chaplains who walk the landings of our prisons or who sit in cramped cells listening tenderly, absolving the sin, guilt and shame, blessing and humbly, wisely receiving. They bring Good News for the poor, they provide an experience of the compassionate heart of God.

"Prison" though, is something within the experience of us all. There is something still holding each of us bound. As a priest, entrusted with the care of souls, I feel unworthy and inadequate, knowing I share in weakness too, just like those in my care. An earthenware jar for sure!

Just occasionally, there is a glimpse into the mystery of that love which is God himself. A love for me, unworthy though I am and for all those I meet, each day. Again R.S. Thomas puts it so well:

> "Prayer like gravel flung at the sky's window,
> Hoping to attract the loved one's attention.
> But without visible plaits to let down for the believer
>   to climb up
> To what purpose open that far casement?
> I would have refrained long since
> But that peering once through my locked fingers
> I thought that I detected the movement of a curtain."

Yet, here I am by the providential care of the Lord, his power manifested in my weakness. All praise to God.

Mgr Malachy Keegan, Principal Chaplain, H.M. Prison Service.

On Not Standing Safe on the Bank

Archbishop Patrick Kelly

Praise to the holiest in the height,
And in the depth be praise;
In all his words most wonderful,
Most sure in all his ways.

The Venerable John Henry Newman

One day I visited the place across the Jordan where John first baptised. Our Lord's baptism had long made a claim on my heart and mind – a claim of loving wisdom, wisest love and praise to the holiest in the height. But the reality of the Jordan flowing slowly, sluggish and meandering, had not thrilled me. Then we came to Elijah's spring – a cauldron of three surging, bubbling, powerful springs. No wonder that St John wrote of John "baptising at Aenon near Salim because water was abundant there" (Jn 3:23).

When I visited the tiny Catholic Church in Iran a genius has designed waters so to flow that, while it was abundant, its surface was so still that fish could be seen dancing in the depths. But the waters at Elijah's, at John's spring are a surging menace, a battering force dealing death as well as life.

There Jesus had been baptised, and in that place is contained my whole life as priest and bishop, for there Jesus did not stand safe, aloof and at a distance from us sinners in all that shatters, batters and kills life in abundance. Being for us Emmanuel, God with us, he did indeed undergo "the double agony in man for man". As we will ponder in Holy Week, the Son of God did not deal with our sins by a word of authority or a gesture of power. No, "he was wounded for our transgressions, and upon him was the punishment that makes us whole. Stricken for the transgressions of his people, he bore the sins of many."

On the eve of Holy Week Jesus went back to the place and many came to him there. In Holy Week we know that "everything that John said about this man was true", and what John said was "Behold, the Lamb of God." Not behold the lion – no, behold the lamb. John testified: "I saw the Holy Spirit come down and overshadow him in the form of a dove." A dove, not an eagle.

Twenty-five years ago today, at the laying on of hands by Bishop Thomas Holland, with Archbishop Derek Worlock on his right and Archbishop Maurice Couve de Murville on his left, hundreds prayed for that same Spirit to overshadow me. They prayed to have formed in me a mind and heart such that I would never stand aloof, safe and untroubled on the bank. They prayed that I would never speak from a distance claiming an authority or power that had not been tested and formed by entering into the seething cauldron of all that stands in the way of life in abundance.

I must one day give an account of whether I have tried to keep as faithful followers of the Lamb who was slain all those to whom I have been sent. I know that the Spirit is with me so that I may encourage priests and deacons to be open to that Spirit, who plunges them into the joys and hopes, the sorrows and sadness of God's own holy people.

I am also certain that the ecumenical journey, so fittingly signified by the monument on Hope Street to Bishop David Sheppard and Archbishop Derek Worlock, cannot be accomplished from a distance, but only by shared prayer, mutual struggling with the word of God and friendship in the Lord.

We cannot bear life in abundance unless, like Nugent Care, we are plunged into the complexity of the life of our city, our country, our world and involved in the economic, commercial, legal, penal and civic activity which is all around us. We must not remain on the bank, safe, aloof, terrible in denunciation and rebuke so that all despair. We must remain true to the words that began Lent and come to their awesome climax in the events of Holy Week, words true of Jesus Christ and to be reflected in us: "For our sake God made him to be sin who knew no sin, so that in him we might become the righteousness of God."

It is so clear. For such wonders "Through him, with him, in him, in the unity of the Holy Spirit, all honour and glory are yours, almighty Father, for ever and ever."

Archbishop Patrick Kelly, Archbishop of Liverpool.

Based on the homily delivered on the occasion of the Silver Jubilee of his Episcopate, 3 April 2009.

People, Priest and the Lord

Mgr Mark Langham

It is dangerous when priests write about priesthood. Some seize the opportunity to justify their own style of ministry; why they meditate in the woods, or wear birettas, or eat tofu. In this case their manifesto will probably be of little interest or value beyond their own fan club. Others write in euphoric tones of priesthood in general that seem quite remote from life, and unlike any priesthood that most of us recognise.

I suspect that you can only begin to describe priesthood truthfully when you are clear about three things: whom it is for, whom it involves, and whom it signifies.

Priesthood (especially diocesan priesthood) is for people. If you doubt this, ask any priest who – like me – is caught up in administration. Detached from immediate contact with those he is called to serve, he finds himself unsustained, unrooted. It is people who ground priests and give them purpose; it is in service of people that the priest finds his fullest joy, his greatest challenges, and his deepest fulfilment.

I have felt this most acutely in moments of transition – notably, weddings and funerals. Although an outsider, the priest is summoned into the circle of intimacy, to be part of the most decisive instances of a life. Whether that be standing with a young couple as they take their marriage vows, or kneeling with a family at the bedside of a dying relative, the priest furnishes the words and actions (and even the silence) that will give eternal meaning to those moments, and hope and comfort to those present. At such times the priest realises he is part of something bigger than his own humanity. So, even (or especially) when caught up in the industry of administration, the priest must regard ministry to people as his natural habitat, the landscape in which his calling makes most sense.

Secondly, priesthood involves the priest himself; I mean by that the whole man – in all his aspects, strengths and frailties. Priesthood is not an occupation requiring distinct proficiency in particular areas; it is a calling that claims every talent and skill the priest possesses – indeed, there is surely no other calling that so resolutely demands all one's gifts.

Accordingly, priesthood is not merely fulfilling, but also endlessly challenging. The priest must spin many plates. He will need to draw upon his own repertoire of skills, both spiritual and secular. He may have to talk a suicide down from a parapet, or iron a basketful of altar linen – and certainly very much in between – but all this gives him a lively sense that he is being moulded, shaped, made into all that he can be. Which is, I would say, another way of talking about happiness.

Thirdly, priesthood signifies Christ. It begins and ends in him, and all this moulding and shaping is Christ's work. A priest does not simply lead others, or tell them what to do; he creates real communion with the Lord – he helps God happen to people. That is the source of his being, and indeed the goal of his life, supremely and astoundingly summed up in his celebration of the Eucharist. For there the priest celebrates, imparts and receives his very Lord; there he shares Christ's sacred ministry and grows in his likeness. Even the greatest and holiest priest feels weak at the knees as he contemplates that.

People, priest and Lord; essential aspects of priesthood that bring together earth and heaven, present and eternity. I can imagine no greater privilege, no deeper joy, and no more awesome responsibility.

Mgr Mark Langham works for the Pontifical Council for the Promotion of Christian Unity at the Vatican.

Taken, Blessed and Broken

Fr Philip Law

Peter: It is misty. We had been out all night and the fishing hadn't been all that successful. There He was standing close to the shore, "Leave your nets behind, come and follow me." What did He mean, no longer fishermen but fishers of men?

So we find ourselves following Him. I often wondered during my life of sharing in His priesthood, having been called to love, to serve, why me? Perhaps it should be why **not** me?

Jesus asked his first apostles, whom He called His friends, "What can you bring to feed the hungry, weary crowd of thousands?" Today we bring the meagre loaves and fishes which He so willingly receives. Once He has taken, blessed and broken in His divine gentleness, everyone is satisfied. There is always more than enough to go around and He gathers up even the scraps, so nothing is wasted.

Being one of his priests, of some thirty two years, I still remember vividly my ordination day and being awoken with a cup of tea and my mother's familiar tone: "Why not go for a little walk? Oh, you might like to take the dog with you." So off I went to Grovelands Park, into the woods and I thought, "Oh God, please help me!" Deep inside I heard those words of consolation: "Do not be afraid, I am with you always…"

These words still echo in my life today. Sometimes I do not listen enough, or when rushing around I simply don't make enough time, for His words to fill me. Neither do I remember to thank Him as often as I should.

Perhaps the whole of our life could be a little personal "thank you" to God; thank you for asking me to be one of your fishermen. The prayer I prayed on the feast of

St Matthias, my ordination day, still resonates with a new strength today, "Oh God, please help me!" The answer is still "Do not be afraid, I am with you always." Now, for me, there is a new intensity to this prayer.

Let us return to the sea of Galilee, to contemplate the breakfast on that first Easter. The charcoal fire was lit and Jesus said "Bring what you have." Later, bringing the catch of the day, Peter is asked "Peter, do you love me? … feed my lambs, feed my sheep, follow me." He continued: "…When you were young you put on your own belt,… but when you grow old you will stretch out your hands and somebody else will put a belt round you and take you where you would rather not go."

I always thought that this passage from the gospel was meant for someone else, but after a slight stroke last year while leading a pilgrimage to the Holy Land it began to dawn on me that though we spend our lives giving of our best in doing the Lord's work, He is asking us "Can you be there for me?" and it is in the "being" rather than "doing" that I find quite a challenge.

Remember, after the laying on of hands, when the bishop and your fellow brother priests greet you and welcome you into a wonderful intimacy that these brothers are and will continue to be a source of inspiration, encouragement and constant support.

Together with our fellow brothers and sisters alike, we share the journey. They teach us repeatedly how the Lord takes, blesses and breaks: "This is my body given for you…" "I am with you always. Do not be afraid."
If lately I have not thanked the one who invited me to follow Him, may I take this opportunity to do so.

Fr Philip Law, Parish Priest of Whetstone, London.

On One's Knees

Mgr Christopher Lightbound

To speak of myself, I suppose that one day I shall really learn the lesson that all success comes from God. It is a bitter lesson, but when human plans and paper strategies fail, when people seem so slow to co-operate, when financial anxieties press heavily, then that lesson must be learnt. It is learnt principally on one's knees. It is humiliating to find that everything we were told in the seminary about the importance of prayer, and which we accepted simply as pious waffle, was true.

Prayer becomes a necessity to the pastoral priest. How much? Not for me the three or four hours daily practised by an earlier writer in this series. Disjointed half-hours here and there are the most that I can rise to. My 'prayer life' is a hotchpotch of dog-eared meditation books, the New Testament, mechanical rosaries, distractions (usually about money) and the occasional flash of inspiration – from my psyche or the Holy Spirit, who knows? I have found recently that my Sunday sermons tend to boomerang on Tuesday or Wednesday, when I suddenly realise that I ought to practise what I preach.

How much of one's prayer and encounter with the Unknown God is self-deception? I ask myself that question from time to time and find that I have no rational answer. There is nothing I can prove. I do not live in the constant presence of God – such graces are for souls more choice and purified than I. But there is a self-evident, self-authenticating power in the life of faith. I can say with St Paul: "I know whom I have believed", and at the same instant realise that I do not really know him. He eludes my human comprehension; he vanishes when I think I can picture him – or rather the prefabricated picture vanishes, and he remains, transcendent but beckoning. And the search begins again.

Mgr Christopher Lightbound is a retired priest of the Diocese of Shrewsbury.
Extract from his book *The Church Then and Now,* St Pauls Publishing, 2004.

The Partnership of Priest and People

Bishop Bernard Longley

"Every priest relies on the faith and talents of his parish community. If he is wise he will not only know the joy of dispensing God's grace, but also of receiving it abundantly through his parishioners as well. The partnership between priests and people is built upon prayer, collaboration, mutual respect and love."

Pope John Paul II

I heard those words as a newly-ordained priest and they described and illuminated for me what I had always experienced as the characteristic and close relationship between Catholic priests and their people. The experience of this relationship was indeed one of the principal reasons that I had felt drawn towards the priesthood as a way of life long before I came to understand in any detail what priestly life and witness meant. Like so many of my brother priests it was seeing the priesthood in action and experiencing the friendship and support of my own Parish Priest in Manchester that had first awakened a sense of vocation within me.

The text I have quoted comes from the homily preached by Pope John Paul II at the priestly ordination he celebrated in Heaton Park, Manchester during his Pastoral Visit to the UK in May 1982. While it has always been a dimension of the valued relationship between priests and lay-people, our understanding of the giving and receiving described by Pope John Paul deepened through the insights of the Second Vatican Council. Its reflection on the life and ministry of priests, *Presbyterorum Ordinis*, emphasises the priest's capacity and duty to discern and promote the charisms of the laity.

This partnership between priest and people, sometimes referred to as collaborative ministry, is rooted in the nature of Christian priesthood as a sharing in the Priesthood of Christ. The Lord's Priesthood is sacramentally manifest in the Church today through baptism and ordination, in ways which Vatican II teaches us are different not only in degree but in kind, and these manifestations are complementary and mutually enriching. As the charisms of the laity flourish within the Church, vocations to the ordained priesthood should be expected to increase, not to diminish – as vocations to the ordained priesthood thrive – so the gifts of the lay faithful can be more and more discerned and encouraged.

The partnership between priest and people is also implied by the significance the Church gives to the concept of incardination. At ordination we enter into a binding relationship with the local Church, the diocese. Incardination is the canonical embodiment of the theological relationship that holds bishop, priests and deacons together within the diocese. This is further developed in the Code of Canon Law: "Since all clerics are working for the same purpose, namely the building up of the body of Christ, they are to be united with one another in the bond of brotherhood and prayers. They are to seek to cooperate with one another." (275 §1)

Insofar as incardination describes the priest's relationship with his diocese it also involves the bonds that unite him with all the faithful of the diocese, and in particular with those whom he serves and with whom he shares day by day in the community of the parish or chaplaincy. This community is the setting in which every priest is expected to discern and promote the charisms of the lay-faithful for the good of the whole People of God.

When I was preparing for priestly ordination in the early 1980s a priest of my diocese offered some advice. With his characteristic mixture of kindness and candour he said: 'Bernard, don't become one of those efficient types!'

For some time I was mystified by what he could mean – I had always been encouraged to use whatever vision, ability or energy I had to the Church's best advantage. Gradually I saw that I was being discouraged from trying to be so effective in my ministry that I overlooked or left little room for the vision, ability or energy of others, especially among the laity.

In his homily in Manchester, Pope John Paul also said: "… *the Church must be a family – bishops, priests, deacons, religious and laity, supporting each other and sharing with each other the individual gifts given by God.*" Good parents love to see their children flourish and this must be reflected in the family of the Church. As priests we live our vocation most authentically when, in the Eucharist, we can give thanks to God for the charisms which He has enabled to be more and more fruitful in the lives and witness of the lay-faithful through our own ministry.

Bishop Bernard Longley, Auxiliary Bishop of Westminster.

A Beautiful Ministry

Fr Flor McCarthy SDB

Of all the stories in the Gospel the following is my favourite, and if there is one story that captures the essence of our ministry it is surely this.

On Easter Sunday evening two sad and forlorn disciples of Jesus were returning home to Emmaus, a village about seven miles from Jerusalem. They had firmly believed that Jesus was the promised Messiah. But when he was crucified their hopes went up in smoke. A crucified Messiah was a contradiction in terms.

Their idea of the Messiah was that of an all-conquering hero, who would restore Israel to its former greatness. This was not Jesus' idea of the Messiah. On more than one occasion he had tried to tell his disciples that the Messiah would suffer and be put to death, but they didn't want to know.

They made their way homewards, sad at heart and down in spirit. At a certain point a stranger joined them. "What were you talking about as you walked along?" he asked in a kindly manner. With that they poured out their sad story to him.

They told him all about Jesus of Nazareth, and the great things he had said and done among the people. They told him how the chief priests arrested him, and handed him over to the Romans who crucified him three days previously.

They told him that early that morning some women disciples had gone to his tomb and found it empty, and claimed they had seen angels who declared that he was alive. Some of their friends had gone to the tomb and found that what the women said was true, but of him they saw nothing.

"You foolish men!" the stranger said. "So slow to

believe all that the prophets had said! Did you not know that the Messiah *had* to suffer in order to enter into his glory?"

Then he opened their minds to a new way of looking at the Scriptures. He showed them how all the prophets from Moses onwards had foretold that the Messiah would suffer, and thus enter into glory.

The two listened with rapt attention. So absorbed were they in what the stranger was saying that they didn't feel the miles going by. Before they knew it, they had reached Emmaus. By this time night was falling, but he made as if to go on. They invited him to stay with them, and he agreed to do so.

Later, when they were having supper, he took the cake of bread, blessed it, broke it, and gave each of them a piece – just as Jesus had done at the Last Supper.

Suddenly their eyes were opened and they recognised the stranger. He was none other than Jesus! But at that moment he disappeared from their sight.

Then they said to one another, "We should have known all along that it was he! Were not our hearts burning within us as he explained the Scriptures to us?"

In spite of the lateness of the hour, they set off back to Jerusalem to share the good news with the apostles. Their beloved Jesus was alive, and had entered into glory!

And what was that glory? It was his triumph over evil and death. So the death of Jesus, far from being the end of the dream, was precisely the way it was realised. Jesus was the Messiah, not in spite of his suffering, but because of it.

What is our task as priests except to accompany people, often on sad and lonely roads, to listen to them, to explain the scriptures to them, and to help them recognise their risen Lord in the breaking of the Eucharistic bread. Is there a more beautiful ministry?

Fr Flor McCarthy SDB, Dublin.

Disciples of Christ

Fr Liam McCarthy OFM

"When times are hard and difficult, remember the joy of these days."

These were the words of Pope Paul VI. We, the newly ordained, had an audience with him; so many years ago – forty-five! The joy of those far off days comes back, as to the mind of Wordsworth: "…in vacant or in pensive mood they flash upon that inward eye, which is the bliss of solitude." The joy of those days, the kneeling in the sanctuary, the Litanies being sung (*Sancta Maria ora pro eis*), the chant of the *Veni Creator* and the words of the Bishop, "O God, source of all holiness, fountain of true consecration and fullness of benediction, pour down, Lord, on these thy servants whom we are dedicating to the honourable office of the priesthood, the gift of thy blessing. May they, by the dignity of their behaviour and the pattern of their lives, show themselves true elders, moulded by the teaching that Paul gave to Titus and Timothy. May they, by day and night, ponder on the law, believe what they read, teach what they believe, practise what they preach."

It all took place in Rome and now I find myself in Africa as a Missionary. I thank God for the vocation he gave me. There have been so many moments of joy – the offering of Mass, preaching the Word, administering the Sacraments, especially the Sacrament of Reconciliation – aware always of being a "vessel of clay". But, like the Disciples on the road to Emmaus "Were not our hearts burning within us as He spoke to us on the road?" Looking back over the years of travelling that Road to Emmaus the supportive love of so many people is something very precious.

The call to the Priesthood is rooted in the personal

friendship of Jesus. The Master calls. Into the vineyard we go and accept that part of the vineyard allotted to us. For some it may be the vineyard of sickness and suffering, for others it may be the vineyard of misunderstanding, for others the vineyard of the "dark night of the soul" and for all, the vineyard of the mercy and love of God. At all times in the vineyard we hear the words of Jesus, "You have not chosen me. I have chosen you. I call you friends."

Looking back and reflecting, I see, in the Gospel, that Jesus firstly TAUGHT the disciples; on the Mount of Beatitudes, in the parables and especially by His example. He then formed them into a COMMUNITY with the command "Love one another as I have loved you." Thirdly, he MISSIONED them, sent them out to "Go and teach all nations…". This threefold dynamic – Teaching, Community, Mission – is, in a special way, the journey of the priesthood. Jesus teaches us in so many ways and we are always learning to listen to Him, especially in prayer. "Lord teach us how to pray". We have been called into Community, "sharing the one bread and the one cup" with our fellow priests, the faithful, all the community of believers in the bonds of friendship. Then we are sent to bring joy, peace, hope and healing to many along the way, but first we are sent into the depths of our own hearts to be renewed deep down as authentic preachers of the Word, with kindness and compassion.

As we celebrate the Eucharist, the Liturgy of the Word is our teaching. We are "taught by the Word", and respond "Speak Lord, your servant is listening." The Liturgy of the Eucharist forms us all into a community. Eucharistic Prayer 3 says: "Grant that we, who are nourished by his body and blood, may be filled with his Holy Spirit, and become one body, one spirit in Christ." We are then sent: "Go in peace to love and serve the Lord." Our lives become truly Eucharistic as we live out the Eucharist as the friend of Jesus who came to "serve and not to be served." He changed the water into wine at Cana when those who drew the water had "done whatever he told them". Mary, Mother of all priests, has the same words for us "Do whatever he tells you." We give him what we have and, as water was changed into wine at Cana, we too are changed and renewed by the power of the Spirit. Yes, as we remember the joy of that day, the day of Ordination, we too will continue on the road as evening comes, aware that Jesus walks by our side with love and compassion. May the words of Richard of Chichester keep us always generous in the service of the Lord:

"What I spent I had, what I kept I lost,
but what I gave, I have."

Fr Liam McCarthy OFM works in Zimbabwe.

The Kenosis of Preaching

Fr Enda McDonagh

I take as my model for the priest in preaching, that developed by Paul on the self-implying (kenosis) of Christ in his Letter to the Philippians (chapter 2). The broader treatment in the article as a whole gives a better understanding.

Surrender to the scriptures of the day is an obvious demand for an authentic homily. Some of these readings are prescribed or selected as appropriate to the occasion, be it Easter Day or Wedding Day. So preparation for the particular liturgy, remote and immediate, already includes their inhabiting one's mind and heart. Yet their broader biblical and theological contexts in the Old and New Testament, as well as in the later tradition, should form the implicit if unspoken background out of which the congregation on this particular occasion is addressed. As both Easter and Wedding Celebrations are primarily celebrations of new life, they might carry biblical echoes of other great celebrations from Creation to Exodus, from Bethlehem to Cana to Emmaus, from Isaiah's depiction of the banquet which the Lord is preparing for his people to Ezekiel's vision of the Valley of the Dry Bones to the new heavens and the new earth promised in the Book of Revelation. For weddings in particular the innumerable biblical variations on the themes of divine and human love should, if not explicitly expressed in the readings chosen, be close to the surface of the homilist's thought and word. In the actual homily the richness of the unspoken background may be more influential than the readings or more explicit citations from the scriptures.

Influential with whom? With the particular congregation assembled about the preacher first of all, and perhaps less directly with their families and friends. (Some people still speak of good and bad sermons they have recently heard.) The liturgical occasion with its scriptural readings leads to the more profound and mysterious kenosis of the preacher before the preached to, the actual congregation on the day. For that to happen he must know them, not all or perhaps any of them personally, although knowing some of them should be the norm, but he must know them in their general background and common humanity, in their gender, ethnic, cultural, economic, professional and age diversity, in their shared joys and griefs, hopes and fears. Much of this may be gleaned from his previous encounters with similar people as well as from the stories of his own life and that of his family and friends. Yet he must consider each congregation anew, even his regular Sunday congregation, which he only gradually gets to know well and which in any case is always changing, however slightly, in its composition and in individual lives. It is into these lives that he must empty himself and his faith, hope and love in words prompted – perhaps even inspired, by the liturgical occasion and its scriptures. Such self-emptying may have its shadow-side for the assembly through his weaknesses or theirs, but it will avoid mastering the congregation in any exhibitionist or prideful way. Mastery is not the role of the Christian preacher but humble service.

Fr Enda McDonagh is a priest of the Archdiocese of Tuam.

Taken from an article which appeared in *The Furrow* January 2009.

A Personal Reflection on the Priesthood

Archbishop Kevin McDonald

The current world financial crisis has shown how fragile are the institutions on which we depend for our security and prosperity. It has been quite a shock. I think that the uncertainty and insecurity now evident in our financial institutions reflect something in our society as a whole, namely a lack of secure and trustworthy institutions in which people can really put their faith. Related to this is a strong sense many people have that we live in something of a moral and spiritual vacuum. Certainly people tend to be both critical and sceptical of those who hold any kind of moral or spiritual authority. It is a culture in which "choice" is paramount but we may wonder about what values and principles inform peoples' choices. I want to suggest that precisely in this kind of society a Catholic priest has a vital role and one that is uniquely fulfilling and rewarding.

There is something absolute about priesthood, something which runs directly counter to the prevailing culture. The most important task a priest has is to celebrate the Eucharist. In doing this, he situates himself within a tradition of worship that reaches back in history, to long before the development of our modern culture and ethos. The Eucharist finds its roots in the Old Testament and finds its meaning in the death and resurrection of Christ. Jesus Christ was and is the Saviour of the world and the fruits of his saving death are made available at every Mass under the forms of bread and wine. As the ordinary minister of baptism, it is the priest who brings people into a personal relationship with Christ. When he celebrates the sacrament of reconciliation, he provides the forgiveness that enables people to restore and heal that relationship insofar as it has been damaged through sin.

The priest, therefore, is a sure and reliable reference

point. His ministry provides *life* – life which brings stability here and now as well as hope for eternal life. In himself, the priest enjoys a deep confidence about the value of his role and his work in the world. It is a confidence grounded in faith, nourished by hope, and expressed in love of people, especially those entrusted to his care. The presence of a priest in a local community provides a level of security that no political organisation or social service can provide.

The Year of the Priesthood that has been proclaimed by Pope Benedict is a wonderful opportunity to celebrate the gift of priesthood. The paradox of a priest's life is that although he lives with constraints that many find not only hard but hard to understand – obedience, celibacy – these very constraints create the conditions for a life of freedom and availability that is quite special. In 1968 when I applied to train for the priesthood in my home diocese of Birmingham, I was interviewed by Archbishop George Patrick Dwyer. As I was leaving his office after the interview he looked up at me and said, "Kevin, priesthood is the best life in the world. Nothing can touch it – provided you give yourself to it completely." I have always remembered those words. We need to give our whole selves to God in the priesthood. Whatever we hold back will become a burden to us.

It is in the ministry to people that the priest finds happiness and is most at home and most himself. Central to the secret of priesthood is drawing life from our ministry to others. In the year dedicated to the priesthood, we should pray that priests will manifest the joy and freedom that is proper to their calling in such a way that others will see it and some will wish to share in it themselves.

Archbishop Kevin McDonald, Archbishop of Southwark.

Building Up God's People

Bishop Malcolm McMahon OP

All priests are called to "bring the people of God into being and increase it". This seems so daunting. Hasn't it already been done? The new covenant established by our Lord has been preached and announced in our world. Why is it then that so often our task seems to be to build community? Some people remember fondly the good old days when being a catholic meant being part of a strong, clearly identifiable community, full of confidence. Can we recreate that kind of community? I do not think so. Anyway, our mission should be to build up communion not simply community. Building community is one thing but building communion is another. When we use the phrase "God's people" we mean not just any group of people but those who are baptised into Christ. So one answer to this nagging command that will never go away, "to bring into being God's people", is to baptise, reconcile and feed his people with the divine food. But there is much more to building up of the people of God.

Sometimes you hear priests having a little moan. I remember meeting a priest friend of mine in London at his church. He had enormous bunch of keys in his hand – he had just been locking up the parish hall. "I wasn't ordained to be a caretaker", he grumbled. "Of course you were", I replied, quick as a flash. What I meant to do was to emphasise that flowing directly from his ordination was this duty, command, dare I say power, to build up God's people. As a priest you give what it takes precisely because you were ordained for it.

Let me try to put that another way. Once soon after I was ordained, I came from the altar after a pretty appalling liturgy – the cantors annoyed everyone by waving their arms about and singing out of tune, the thurifer upset the thurible and burnt a hole in the carpet, there was general chaos amongst the altar servers and you could see the look of boredom on the faces of the people. A visiting priest from Australia said, "Malcolm, when liturgy fails put the people on a bus and drive them into the outback." Well, I didn't drive them into the bush but I put them on a bus and took them to Rome, Lourdes, Rimini, Ireland, Austria, Spain – even Eurodisney! This was one of many ways that I started building community – bringing God's people into being. It is hard work making community, but what makes it communion? As baptised people we live not for ourselves but for others. That is the key to understanding how a community can be transformed into communion. Baptised people have Christ at their centre, and the priest represents Christ. He stands in his stead. Where he stands there also is Christ. That is why the local model railway club may provide a lot of what we know as community but can never be communion. That is why I could say to my fed-up priest friend in London that he was ordained to carry a big bunch of keys and call the bingo at the old folks club on a Tuesday afternoon. By his presence he transformed those meetings. We have to remember that by virtue of his ordination a priest has been ordained to lead, and he leads through service, in the manner of our Lord. Ordinary, everyday tasks are part of his mission. These are important elements in building up the people of God and giving it increase.

Bishop Malcolm McMahon OP, Bishop of Nottingham.

Sons of Encouragement

Bishop Thomas McMahon

The Year of the Priesthood proclaimed by the Holy Father is, also, special in a personal way because November 2009 sees the 50th anniversary of my own ordination to the priesthood. I rejoice to say that during my ministry as both priest and bishop I have been constantly sustained and guided by many words of encouragement. Sometimes these words have been spoken – by clergy and religious, by family and friends and, so often, by the people of the parishes where I have served as priest and, as bishop, by the people of the Diocese, whom I have met in so many ways. Equally, such words have come to me in written form – from books and homilies and articles, the fruit of pastors and writers who give witness to the whole spectrum of our rich Christian tradition.

I find it significant that in the Ordination Rites of a number of the Eastern Churches, the principal gift prayed for in the Prayer of Consecration is that of "encouragement". This is an inspiring reminder of how much an ordained minister is called to be filled with this gift and of how central it is to our ministry. Through this insight we are aware of the call to turn day by day to the Lord so that He may renew this spirit within us both as a person and as a priest; in turn, we are then empowered to bring fresh heart to those entrusted to our care.

Several years ago, I remember being particularly struck by some words of the late Cardinal Bernardin, Archbishop of Chicago. He was talking about what people expect from their priests. He said that what people actually want and need from us is usually less complex or spectacular than what we might imagine. In short, God's people are not looking to us as someone with all the answers to life's questions and problems; in fact already they either have a clear awareness of the answer themselves or have enough innate good sense to appreciate that there is no easy answer. Instead, said the Cardinal, what they want is for us to be present to them and to pray with them: "More than anything else people look to us who minister to them for our presence as loving, caring and forgiving people… they want someone who will pray with them, whose presence will remind them that no matter what their difficulties might be, God really loves them and cares for them." We have become priests because we know instinctively that this is what we want to do. It is a simple, profound and deeply rewarding calling.

People with little experience of the Church sometimes think that a priest's existence is one that is rarefied and doesn't actually engage with reality. As priests, we know this is simply not the case. By being a priest, we have a special place in the lives of our people, whether in times of their greatest joys or sorrows, as well as in the week by week living out of ordinary life, with all its blessings and challenges – few others have this great privilege. Through our ministry we are blessed to see the action of God and His grace at work in the lives of those whom we serve. This then becomes a source of great encouragement for us. During this Year of the Priesthood, let us ask the Lord to make each one of us more and more a true Barnabas, a "son of encouragement".

Bishop Thomas McMahon, Bishop of Brentwood.

The Monastic Life

Abbot Cuthbert Madden OSB

My first contact with the Benedictines of Ampleforth Abbey came in 1976. I was a medical student in London and I had heard that Abbot Basil Hume was to be ordained to serve as Archbishop of Westminster. I had never seen anyone ordained so I went, stood at the back of that immense Cathedral and watched and prayed.

Six years later I was wondering what to make of my life. I was enjoying working as a doctor in Bath but felt that there was something missing. I had read "Searching for God" but it had not made any great impact on me. I found myself continuing to pray the Prayer of the Church and reflecting on the Sacred Scripture set for the Sunday Mass. I started writing some of these reflections into a journal. I had found my way, in fact, to *lectio divina* though I had never heard of it by this name. On Trinity Sunday of that year, 1982, I found myself in the Abbey Church at Ampleforth and I felt that this was a significant moment, though I did not know why. Two years later I entered the noviciate. In 2005 I was elected to serve the community as their Abbot.

I am often asked what sustains those of us who try to serve the Lord as priests or as monks. It seems to me that there are four strands which weave through our lives: a personal relationship with the Lord which is nourished by prayer and *lectio divina*, the sacramental life of the Church, service of those entrusted to our care and friendship. These have carried me through twenty-five years of monastic life and I pray that they will sustain me to my end.

Of the four the personal relationship with the Lord is paramount. This is the least tangible of the strands and so is most easily neglected. When we devote time to prayer and *lectio* we may find that both can become very dry, very boring. We place ourselves before the Lord to pray and find that we are plagued by distractions or overcome by the desire to sleep. We open our bible or some other spiritual book and find ourselves confronted by words, thousands of words. Yet, if we persevere, occasionally we become aware that we are being called by name, affirmed in terms too personal to be described with any clarity. Our fidelity to prayer is not entirely a personal matter. As a teacher in our school I was struck by the clarity of vision of some of my students who knew when prayer was not a central feature in my life. If we are to have anything to give the people we are called to serve we must set aside time to be given gifts by God. If we rely on our own strengths we quickly find that we are out of our depth and have little to hand on to others.

How the sacraments have the effect they do is a mystery to me, but I have seen the profound effect which can result from their reverent and prayerful celebration. As a monk my experience is much less than that of many others – and yet even here I have seen how the Lord desires to make himself available to people through the words and actions of ordinary men who have dedicated themselves to his service.

In my monastic life I have discovered the transformative effect of the people one is sent to serve. My life has been changed by them – and usually for the better. In the monastic life one does not choose the brethren – God chooses them. In our monastery one does not choose one's work – one is asked to undertake a task. It is astonishing the transformation which can be brought about by the people who are associated with a given ministry of service. I have set out with the notion that I will minister to this group and have found instead that I am the recipient of their ministry. The same is true in the current ministry of service to which I have been committed by my brethren.

Lastly I would want to assert the importance of friendship – a virtue which is under terrible strain in today's world: for if a priest has friends the tongues begin to wag. Yet my experience in the monastery is that friendship is one of the most important means by which we remain human; through true friends we can learn the truth about ourselves, encounter the touch of God and be sustained in his service.

I close by suggesting that the life of a monk-priest is a living act of faith. Nothing I have said makes any sense if one does not believe in a personal God who chooses and commissions people to go out and do his work. We cannot measure the effect of our lives in some easy and straightforward way. We have to be men living in joyful hope of the last times when God's loving purpose is revealed and we will understand the great mystery in which we have played our part.

Abbot Cuthbert Madden OSB, Abbot of Ampleforth.

Put Out Into the Deep

Archbishop Joseph Marino

"Cast your net over the right side of the boat and you will find something" (Jn 21:6).

These words, from the Gospel of John, in many ways, represent the Easter command of Christ to be brave, dynamic and energetic in our lives as fishers of men. The apostles at this point were most likely still confused and disillusioned, closed within themselves. They were still trying to grasp the reality of the resurrection, not to mention its consequences in their lives.

Their disappointment was made even worse when, resorting to their former work as fishermen, they could not make a good catch of fish. Then the Risen Lord appears and tells them to throw their nets into the deep, and John relates "so they cast them and were not able to pull them in because of the number of fish" (Jn 21:7).

Dear Bishop and priests, these words are addressed to us today. The Lord who is risen from the dead invites us to "put out into the deep" (Lk 5:4). It is an invitation to share in the missionary mission of Our Lord, that is "to go into the whole world and preach the Gospel to mankind" (Mk 16:15).

These words of Christ resonate within our hearts and they form the consequence and goal of our vocation. On 16 March 2009, Pope Benedict XVI, in speaking to the Congregation for the Clergy, spoke about the missionary dimension of the priesthood. In reflecting upon the missionary aspect of our vocation, he said that while the call that we have received is personal, it is not for our person in itself, much less for personal gain. Rather, it is a call to go outside of ourselves towards others. Every vocation is missionary in nature, because the Church herself is missionary.

In so doing, we go to others without fear or trepidation. We go forth with absolute confidence because we know that Christ is with us and the message proclaimed is rooted "in spirit and truth". As a result, we should be zealous and active in all that we undertake, confident that our actions, which come from Christ within us, will transform the lives of those whom we touch and even the communities where we dare to go.

Moreover, we are not bringing just a message of words or a communication of doctrine and not even the writings of a holy book. No, we are bringing a person who is the message, the announcement and the Word which became flesh. We are bringing Christ, true God and true man, the Risen Lord who is alive and living in the Church and in the hearts of people who desire the good.

The Pope also said to the Congregation for the Clergy: "The mission is 'ecclesial' because no one proclaims himself in the first person, but within and through his own humanity every priest must be well aware that he is bringing to the world Another, God himself. God is the only treasure which ultimately people desire to find in a priest."

Very simply put, we bring God to others, and all people are searching for him. The message of Easter is comforting and powerful: "Do not be afraid or confused and do not stay closed within yourselves." Rather, go to those when the occasion arises and be men of God; let your presence reflect the presence of God and, if asked, simply tell those whom you meet that God is love and our way of life is defined by love.

To be faithful missionaries, because that is exactly what we are, we must be one with Christ. We must have an intimacy with Christ which comes from the daily formation of our spiritual lives, through our prayer, our meditation, examination of conscience and above all in our celebration of the Eucharist where today the Risen Lord comes to us in the appearance of bread and wine.

Archbishop Joseph Marino, Apostolic Nuncio to Bangladesh.
Homily at a gathering of Priests, Mymensingh, Bangladesh, Easter Friday, 17 April 2009.

Thoughts on the Priesthood

Bishop John Mone

My mother did not want me to be a priest. She prayed: "Dear Lord you have given me four sons; take three to serve you as priests but don't take John – he would not be strong enough." It was only after I was ordained that I learned this.

What's more my father advised me to "Say three Hail Marys every day that you will not be chosen as a bishop. To be a priest is awesome enough, but the responsibility a bishop has to carry is too great." I did not say those Hail Marys!

I have been a priest for fifty-seven years and have never regretted my decision. I ministered happily in parishes for thirty-two years and when I was invited to become a bishop I did not want to lose that closeness to people. At first I asked: "Can I refuse?" After prayer I realised it was not my will but "Thy will be done."

In this year dedicated to "The Priesthood", I am becoming more aware that God lives and acts through his priests. Pope Benedict said it beautifully in the Mass of Chrism in 2007: "He anoints the hands of a priest to pass on his Divine Touch."

The Mass of Chrism, celebrated each year in Holy Week, has meant so much to me each year since it was introduced in 1955. It highlights the union between each priest and his bishop, between all priests and bishops throughout the world and between the faithful people and their bishops. The priests renew the commitment of service made at ordination when they were called "to serve and not be served". The "Preface of the Priesthood" sums up for me the priestly vocation. "Christ with a brother's love chooses men to share his sacred ministry. He appoints them to renew in his name the sacrifice of our redemption.

He calls them to lead your holy people in love, nourish them by your word and strengthen them through the sacraments. They are to give their lives in your service and for the salvation of your people, as they strive to grow in the likeness of Christ and honour you by their courageous witness of faith and love."

Such has been my affection for this Preface that I chose from it the words "To lead in love" as my Episcopal motto.

The high ideal proposed in the Preface can be achieved only by prayer. I was told in seminary in Paris: "If you do not want to pray, do not become a priest, your life of service and of celibacy will not survive without it." Prayer is an integral part of priestly life. It is not easy, but St Paul and many other saints tell us that we must never stop trying.

At ordination, the bishop stretches out his hands and prays that the man before him will never be the same again once he has received this Sacrament. He will be different and because of that he will make a difference to people's lives.

Priestly celibacy is one of those differences. The world and the media do not understand how a man could choose the celibate life but let no priest ever undervalue the witness it gives to an unconvinced world. Celibacy is a priest's gift back to God, not to deny love but to open his heart to a greater love by which he will father people into eternal life and, like Mary, give birth to Jesus in their heart.

As a bishop I have visited many Primary schools. If I ask the children what they are good at they find it hard to answer. They think they are not good at anything but once prompted they realise they are good at something, be it running, football, spelling, netball and so on. One little boy told me he was good at making people laugh. I said that being a young comedian was a great talent and asked him how he did it. He replied: "I tickle them!"

I enjoy sharing my love of music with others. During those school visits I would play the piano, perhaps a favourite hymn and then some jazz. I would play songs like Boyzone's, "No matter what they tell you, what you believe is true" to encourage them to believe the people who loved them not what others told them. I used the Abba/Westlife song: "I had a dream" to explain the line: "I believe in angels".

Being a bishop and President of Scottish Catholic International Aid Fund has given opportunities to reach out to some of the poorest people in the world. These people often said to me: "Please thank your people for helping us to help ourselves. We do not want to be beggars. Especially please thank them for sending you. It makes us feel special and important." In a remote area of Africa the people sang: "You are the first bishop since the beginning of creation to visit us!"

The priest's task is to bring God to people and people to God. The most beautiful thing he will do is to bring Jesus to the altar and to the people of God as he celebrates the Holy Sacrifice of the Mass.

Bishop John Mone, Bishop Emeritus of Paisley, Scotland.

50th Anniversary of Priesthood

Cormac Cardinal Murphy-O'Connor

As I look back on fifty years of priesthood I can say, "What marvels the Lord worked for me. Indeed I was glad." My eyes were opened to the light of faith in my Baptism and in the Holy Eucharist so many years ago. My eyes, too, were opened to truth and the example of Jesus my Saviour by the example of others: my parents, my wider family, my community, which is the Church of Jesus. "What marvels the Lord worked for us. Indeed we were glad."

But for me, particularly, on this anniversary of my priesthood, how can I give thanks for the marvels the Lord worked for me as a priest? It is, and has always been the Lord's work. In the letter to the Hebrews today we hear, "No one takes this honour on himself but each one is called by God. Nor did Christ himself give himself the glory of becoming High Priest but he had it from the One who said to him, "You are my Son. Today I have become your Father. You are a priest of the Order of Melchizedek and for ever."

On the day of my ordination I knew that through the sacrament I was receiving I was being signed with a special character and united to Christ the High Priest in such a way that I was able to act in the very person of Christ, the Head of the Church. I was ordained to preach the Gospel, to celebrate the sacraments and to shepherd the faithful people of God. Above all, I recognised on that day that my priesthood was not for myself but for others and that it was to be a life of service to the People of God. For that I dedicated my life. So, indeed, I can say today, "What marvels the Lord worked for me. Indeed I was glad." Glad, because in spite of my weaknesses and sins, that I have been able to render some service to the People of God over so long a time.

So as I speak to you on this day, the anniversary of the day when I celebrated my first Mass, I think I would like to say that the life of a priest is, can and should be a worthy one and a happy one. I have never regretted my decision to be a priest. I hope and trust the Lord will give me grace to persevere to the end. I believe that the vocation of a priest is a precious gift for the Church. But it makes demands on the man who gives himself to it. St Paul says in his letter to the Thessalonians, that he "handed over to God's people and to the Church, not only the Good News, but his whole life as well" (1 Thess 2:8). That is what a priest is called to do. He must in an extraordinary way 'put on Christ', be like Him. By his words and example he must show Christ to others. All I can say is that this task is worth doing and I think that there are many young men in our Church who are ready to hear that call. A vocation is a call, not just from the Church but from God directly to a human soul. It takes time for a man to work it out and for the Church to verify it.

Vocations have not dried up. The faith has not dried up. The hope that is in Christ has not dried up. It is there, still in our midst. "What marvels the Lord works for us. Indeed we were glad." Has it been worthwhile? I believe the answer is "Yes". In the words of the Irish poet Padraic Pearse, "I have squandered the splendid years which the Lord God gave to my youth – in attempting impossible things, deeming them alone worth the toil. Lord, if I had the years I would squander them over again. I fling them from me." Oh, yes, it is worth it and today I give thanks to God for all his goodness and mercy to me over the past fifty years.

Cormac Cardinal Murphy-O'Connor, Archbishop Emeritus of Westminster.

Homily given in Westminster Cathedral, Sunday 29 October 2006.

Forever Young?

Bishop Donal Murray of Limerick

Priests sometimes complain that, because so few are following in our footsteps, we are doomed to be "young priests" for the whole of our lives. Thinking of ourselves as perpetually young might not be such a bad place to start. The best may be yet to come: "There is more felicity on the far side of baldness than young men can possibly imagine" (*Afterthoughts*, Logan Smith).

In the Tridentine Rite the priest begins Mass by announcing that he is going to the altar of God, "to God who gives joy to my youth" (Ps 43:4). Perhaps youth and joy are not the first words that spring to mind when we think of priests today. This is not how it should be. There is a sense in which the Church is supposed to be old and wise and a vigilant guardian of the treasure she has received, but there is another very important sense in which the Church is supposed to be for ever young and joyful, for ever seeking new ways to carry out her mission. The poet Guillaume Apollinaire wrote; "Alone in Europe, oh Christian faith, you are not ancient" ('Zone', Selected Writings).

The ordained ministry should have something of what Pope Paul VI called "the soaring impulse" of youth:

> As long as she remains true to her being and her mission, how could she fail to recognise herself in those who feel themselves to be the bearers of life and hope and of the task of ensuring that there will be a tomorrow for the history of today. (*Gaudete in Domino*, 6)

The truth is, however, that talk about "soaring impulses" is likely to make us feel even wearier than we already are! In our darker moments we may see ourselves as desperately trying to slow down an inevitable decline and hoping that "things may last my time".

Perhaps that tone of desperation and our constant rushing around is the real problem. The source of Christian joy and freshness is the presence of the Risen Christ: "The disciples were filled with joy on seeing the Lord, and he said to them again, "Peace be with you" (Jn 20:20-21). Joy comes from recognising that he is present in every event, every corner and moment of life and everywhere drawing creation to himself. Every tiniest scrap of our lives is filled with the promise of God who makes all things new (Rev 21:5).

Too often we live at a pace that does not allow us to recognise the Lord in all of these presences and to draw strength from him. We carry out all too well the bit about working as if everything depends on us. What we need to learn is to pray as if everything depends on God – which, of course, it does!

We need to make room for what Pope John Paul called 'a contemplative outlook' which sees life in "its utter gratuitousness, its beauty and its invitation to freedom and responsibility" and which "accepts it as a gift" (*Evangelium Vitae*, 83). This outlook can only lead to "songs of joy and thanksgiving for the priceless gift of life" and for the mystery of our call to share in God's unending newness and joy.

Bishop Donal Murray, Bishop of Limerick.

The Preacher

Fr Paul Murray OP

With those friends who disclaim all knowledge
of God, I boast and I say,
"I know Him",
and I say I am speaking from my own experience.
But my friends say: "Be reasonable, how
can you know Him, how can you be so sure
that you are not self-deceived?" This question,
I know is honest, and I know it demands
for an answer not these obscure words
about experience, but the clear evidence
of a man's life. However, I will say it
here again, and even to my own doubting heart
and to my five agnostic senses: "I know Him".

Fr Paul Murray OP teaches at the Angelicum University in Rome.

The Hands of a Priest

Archbishop Vincent Nichols

In this ceremony of priestly ordination, it is the hands of the priest which are anointed. From this day on, these hands will be raised in prayer and entreaty at the altar, on behalf of the people. These hands will be held out in invocation of the Holy Spirit so that our offerings of bread and wine may become the Body and Blood of Christ. These hands will lift before us that same saving presence of Christ. And God will use these hands to impart on us his blessing as the Mass is ended.

In the Sacrament of Reconciliation, the hands of the priest are raised in absolution, bringing the cleansing of our sins and the restoration of peace in our hearts. These hands will anoint the sick and the dying.

In all these gestures, the hands of the priest act for Christ. It is as if he, the priest, has given his hands to Christ for him to use as his own. Just as in Baptism we are entrusted by the Father into the hands of Christ, so too Christ uses the anointed hands of the priest so that he can tend us and fulfil the tasks given to him by the Father.

For these reasons there has long been a custom of not only receiving the first blessing of a newly ordained priest, but also of kissing his hands. The oil of chrism is still fresh on those hands. Christ has just made them his own. Over the years ahead they will be used in all the outward signs of the hidden grace of the sacraments. They will, of course, also be used for all the normal tasks of life. They will move tables and stack chairs; they will cook and help with the washing up; they will pull out lottery tickets and hand over winnings. The hands of a priest will be shaken by so many, so often, at times of sorrow and in moments of celebration. They will wave greetings across the street and knock on countless doors. They will flit across the computer keyboard, and the TV remote control. No doubt at times, they will be used in actions or gestures which are hurtful and damaging, and the wrongdoing will reverberate all the more strongly because they are the hands of a priest.

But on the day of ordination the hands of the new priest are, for us all, a lovely focus of the promises of God, a symbol of the anointed one, Christ himself, who is always in our midst. These hands, too, are a focus of our joy and of our thankfulness to God, the giver of such good gifts.

Today, as we seek the gift of the Holy Spirit to create a new priest, so too we ask the Lord to renew in each of us the effectiveness of our own anointing. May the power of the Holy Spirit fill our hearts again today. May that Spirit refresh in us the effects of our baptism, enfolding us in the embrace of Christ and emboldening us to be Christian in word and deed. May this Holy Spirit confirm in us the courage to be witnesses to hope in a world that seems to be closing in on itself. May we always point to the horizon of God's promise, the promise of lasting peace for all who love him. We pray for our new priest that he will be a faithful minister to all to whom he is sent, being for them the instrument of God's forgiveness, compassion and love.

Archbishop Vincent Nichols, Archbishop of Westminster.
Based on the homily given at the Ordination to the Priesthood of Richard Scott, 18 December 2004 and reproduced by kind permission of Alive Publishing.

An Ordination to the Priesthood Homily

Bishop Brian Noble

For some reason, Mark, as I was thinking about today, airports came into my mind – places of transition – of arrivals and departures. Not a bad image, perhaps, of what we're now about: *"Let 'Mark' who is to be ordained priest come forward"* ... *"Father, holy mother Church asks you to ordain this man, our brother, for service as priest."* And with those simple words, one journey ends and another begins. Years of discernment – by yourself and by the Church – have finally brought you to this moment of arrival, of "touchdown", and now, through the Rite of Ordination, with feet firmly on the ground, there's departure on a hitherto unknown journey.

Perhaps those words surprise you. Haven't years of study, of prayer, of pastoral involvement paved the way for a smooth transition into Priesthood? One might think so, but the experience of the not so long ordained, suggests otherwise. It would seem that no amount of formation, no matter how thorough, can entirely prepare one for what lies ahead, not least, it seems, because people's expectations, some appropriate and some less so, do, in fact, change once one is ordained. That being so, it's wise to set out on this new journey, ready for the terrain to be not as familiar as one might have imagined.

But secondly, and more significantly, that change in people's expectations can, at its best, help to take us to the heart of Priesthood. Don't those changing expectations arise, in fact, from a sound Catholic instinct, that to be ordained is to assume an entirely new ecclesial role and responsibility? That opening request to the Bishop *"to ordain this man, our brother, for service as a priest"* says it all. To be ordained is to be called forth by the Church to a new and representative role, we're ordained for nothing less than representing Christ the head, to the people who are his body.

So, immediately after hands have been laid upon you, you'll be presented with a chalice and paten, with bread and wine; and along with the Book of the Gospels, given you when you received the Diaconate, these will be what we might call the "tools of the trade". But unlike a craftsman's tools which reflect and are at the service of their user, the paten is for Bread which will become *his* Body. The chalice, for Wine which will become *his* Blood and the Book, not our word but *his*. The tools of our trade are entirely in his service, not ours. Ordination is not for us but for Him and his people.

Not surprisingly, then, what is asked for in the Prayer of Ordination, is not that you'll be an eloquent preacher or effective celebrator of the Liturgy; not that you'll be good with the young or good with the sick and the elderly; what is asked is that first and foremost within you the Spirit of Holiness should be renewed, the reason being that, as your choice of Gospel has reminded us, *"a branch cannot bear fruit all by itself, but must remain part of the vine; neither can you unless you remain in me … Whoever remains in me, with me in him, bears fruit in plenty … Cut off from me you can do nothing"* (Jn 15:4f).

Those, Mark, are telling words with which to set out on this new journey. In a moment you'll express your total commitment to it, while we, your fellow pilgrims, join with the Saints of God in praying for you. Let that be a powerful reminder that you're not setting out alone. You have the love, the support and the prayers of your friends and the warmest of welcomes from the Diocese and its Presbyterate.

Bishop Brian Noble, Bishop of Shrewsbury.

Challenges of an Archbishop

Keith Cardinal O'Brien

"Challenge" is a word which must be in the vocabulary of every bishop and priest at this present time. No one of us can be remote, in an ivory tower, in the Church or in civil society today. Perhaps at one time priests and bishops could be remote – but there is an increased and ongoing challenge to be with one's people and to lead one's people from morning to night.

On my own appointment as Archbishop I chose as my motto words from Psalm 99 "Serve the Lord with Gladness". I said to the Pope's representative at the time that I had thoroughly enjoyed twenty years of priesthood and I looked forward to ongoing service with gladness of God and his people in the years which lay ahead as Archbishop. Looking back now over almost twenty-four years of service as Archbishop, with six of them as Cardinal, I realise that I could not have chosen a better motto! Over those years I have "led" on particular issues – and perhaps they all could be described as being on a "pro-life" theme!

Perhaps one of the greatest challenges which I first embraced was no easy one – that of **world poverty**. I experienced poverty on pastoral visits with my priests and people initially in Bauchi in Northern Nigeria and then in El Salvador in Central America – followed by visits to my priests in Chiapas in Mexico and in Guatemala. I was privileged to be one of the leaders of the Make Poverty History Campaign in 2005, leading approximately half a million people, all bearing white armbands, in a great march around the City of Edinburgh. And, of course, my desire to help the poor of the world increased when I was appointed Cardinal in 2003 and became a Director of our Scottish Catholic International Aid Fund (SCIAF) – with further visits to various parts of Africa, including Darfur in the Sudan, and to Asia, including both Cambodia and Myanmar.

The next main pro-life cause which I embraced was the **anti-nuclear campaign**. I worked with very many people in Scotland, including leading representatives of other Churches and political parties in a campaign against the possible renewal of the Trident Nuclear Weapons System, based here in Scotland. In the face of what I had seen as bishop, both in our own country and in most of the countries where I had visited overseas, I could not see any justification at all in the spending of billions of pounds on instruments of mass destruction, which would never ever be used.

Up to the present, the third pro-life theme which I have gladly embraced has been the commemoration of the 40th anniversary of the 1969 **Abortion Act**. The realisation of the evils which have been and still are being perpetrated in our country have not yet sunk in to many of our people. When I used vivid verbal images, I was assailed by very many people in the media but I was able to state that it was not until I used such strong words that any attention had been paid to the statistics about abortion. In a similar manner, I spoke out against the **Human Fertilisation and Embryology Bill** – and was similarly attacked.

It has been and still is a very challenging vocation for me being a pastoral bishop and also a leading figure here in Scotland, whether I like it or not! I regularly think of those words of the great St Paul when he said that we must preach and teach the message of Jesus Christ "in season and out of season, welcome or unwelcome", all supported by a life of prayer and penance, centred on daily Mass and the Sacraments.

It is my hope and prayer now that there may be many more men, young and old, ready to accept the challenge which is facing them to be Christ in the world at this present time.

Keith Cardinal O'Brien, Archbishop of St Andrews and Edinburgh.

Jesus Our Priest

Fr Gerald O'Collins SJ

After several years of joint research, Fr Michael Jones of Huntington, Connecticut, and I have spent this year of St Paul (June 2008 to June 2009) writing a book to be published in 2010 by Oxford University Press, "Jesus Our Priest". The more time we invested in examining the Scriptures and two thousand years of Christian tradition, the more precious themes emerged and took shape for us. Let me share three of our insights into the priesthood of Christ.

First, the Last Supper, crucifixion, resurrection and exaltation into glory unquestionably formed the defining moments in Christ's exercise of his priesthood. Yet the years of his public ministry should also be recognised as priestly. As the Letter to the Hebrews and many great voices in the tradition acknowledged, his priesthood began with the incarnation. He did not become a priest at some later stage, but from the start he already was and acted as a priest. In particular, his public ministry was no "mere" prelude to the exercise of his priesthood. Proclaiming the kingdom, healing the sick, forgiving sinners, feeding the hungry and the other activities that filled the years of Jesus' public life belonged to his priestly ministry as much as his institution of the Eucharist during the celebration of the Last Supper.

Hence St Paul could characterise as a form of priestly liturgy and sacrifice his work of evangelising the Gentiles. In spreading the good news, the Apostle knew himself to be acting as a sacred minister and offering worship to God. Paul "was a minister of Christ Jesus to the Gentiles, in the priestly service of God's gospel" (Rom 15:15-16). When preaching, teaching and pursuing his whole pastoral ministry, Paul was as much a priestly minister as when he baptised some converts (1 Cor 1:16) and presided at the celebration of the Eucharist (Acts 20:7-12).

Second, in celebrating the Eucharist (and, indeed, in further areas of their ministry) ordained priests are visible signs of the invisible, but dynamically present, Christ. At every Eucharist, Christ is the Offerer, the One who invisibly but truly offers the sacramental celebration of his once-and-for-all sacrifice. He takes up into his self-offering the visible priest and the assembled faithful. In the Eucharistic meal he shares himself with all the faithful. The ordained priests act "in the person of Christ" – not in the sense of replacing him or substituting for him but in the sense of acting as visible signs of his invisible and dynamic presence as the Offerer and the Offering. The visible priest presides at the Eucharistic ceremony, but it is Christ who perpetually offers his sacrifice. One might take some famous words of Augustine about baptism and apply them to the Eucharist by saying: "Peter presides, Christ offers. Paul presides, Christ offers."

This truth prompted St Thomas Aquinas to say in a statement quoted by *The Catechism of the Catholic Church* (no. 1545): "only Christ is the true priest, the others being only his ministers". We might gloss this statement and say: only the invisible Christ is the true priest; the others, while visible, are only his ministers.

Third, the priesthood of Christ involved him not only in being tried and tested but also in becoming vulnerable to lethal persecution. Extreme vulnerability belonged to the "job description" of his priesthood provided by the Letter to the Hebrews. His passion and death dramatised the utter vulnerability of his priestly vocation. But his death led to his resurrection and exaltation to the Father's right hand, where he continues eternally his priestly work of self-offering and intercession (Rom 8:34). As Paul put matters, Jesus was "crucified in weakness but now lives by the power of God" (2 Cor 13:4).

In an apostolic and priestly way, Paul himself shared

in that "weakness" and lived by that same "power". Hence he declared: "I am content with weaknesses, insults, hardships, persecutions and calamities for the sake of Christ; for whenever I am weak, then I am strong" (2 Cor 12:10).

Mike Jones and I have become more convinced than ever that any version of the ordained ministry will remain theologically and spiritually impoverished, unless it clearly and constantly draws its reflections from the priesthood of Jesus Christ himself.

Gerald O'Collins SJ is a Jesuit priest.

The Word Becomes Flesh and Lives Among Us

Fr John O'Connor

It is a privilege for me to be a priest. The weekly highlight is the parish Sunday celebration of the Mass.

Every Sunday a diverse group of people gathers for Mass at Our Lady of Victories. Some have been worshipping here for years. They have baptised and married, schooled, partied and prayed together. The young and the old are here. Some are recent arrivals. Others are visiting. All belong. Their hearts carry the deeper richness of human joys, hopes, griefs and anxieties. By the grace and courage of God, I am their priest.

From the sanctuary I see the people as they humbly admit their sin: "I confess to Almighty God, and to you my brothers and sisters that I have sinned, through my own fault…" What a remarkable public confession we make together.

It is our need for God that draws and unites us. Unlike worldly success, this humble starting point is attainable by every honest person. Despite our efforts this past week we have sinned again. This is our reality. Here we again await the real presence of God.

In this restlessness we realise anew that the ultimate in human intimacy is found in communion with other sinners who know God's love. In the sacraments our acknowledged weakness becomes our capacity for God. With these holy people, I am a sinner. For them I am a priest.

The lector proclaims the inspired words of God. In the Gospel we hear that this voice of God has become a person: God in Jesus is the Word, living among us.

Often our minds wander during the readings. Sometimes the playing child distracts the people. At times the microphone lets us down. But always when a sinner listens with hungry heart, Jesus, God's ultimate communication, comes among us to encourage, to comfort and to heal.

Last Sunday I sat down after the homily feeling disappointed. I had not done well. Prayer has not come easily these past weeks and my homily showed it. Then on Tuesday a parishioner who has had an agonising year phoned to thank me for my Sunday homily. She said her burden had lifted for the first time in months and was deeply grateful for what I had said. I was curious and asked which part she had found most helpful. She told me. I knew I had not said what she had heard.

Now we profess our faith. We are not sharing a creed of our own crafting. Instead we announce the faith that is forming us. In a world that labours to create unique belief systems, we stand in a time-tested Tradition and proclaim our sure foundation. God is with us.

As priest I call the people to turn to God in intercessory prayer. Together we articulate the yearnings, hungers, desires and delights of our hearts.

Bread and wine are now brought to the altar. Using me, his priest, God transforms these simple elements. Now the reality of Jesus is tangibly with us in the flesh. Once again, I notice the faces of the people. I see that they recognise this divine presence. Our faith has taught us well. Our lives are now touched again by the ultimate reality.

I offer communion to each person. Jesus allows himself to be given. His flesh becomes our flesh. The people return to their seats in stillness and silent prayer. In these sacred moments we have no doubt of the reality and significance of the miracle that has taken place in our parish church. God has not only come to us. God has come in-to us. The power of this reality casts aside all fear.

It is Sunday night. The people have gone to their homes. Looking back over this day I know again that priesthood is not a job I do but the life I live.

This is life, because the Word has become flesh, and is living among us.

Fr John O'Connor, Parish Priest Our Lady of Victories, Christchurch, New Zealand.

Late Have I Loved Thee

Fr Daniel O'Leary

"Speak to us of God", the cherry tree was asked, and the cherry tree blossomed! My life as a priest was transformed when I began to believe that God was a Lover with a passion for the healing and the blossoming of all people, of all creation.

After decades of clerical ministry I began to realise that what people were yearning for, much more than information about the Church and its doctrines, was the actual redeeming reassurance of God in their daily lives. They wanted the *experience* of God more than knowledge about him. They longed for, in the here and now, hope in their despair, courage in their fear. To be told each Sunday about the utter holiness of their families was the good news they waited to hear. They so sorely needed to be reassured that they are extravagantly and unconditionally loved by a most beautiful God.

The whole enterprise and privilege of being a priest took on a radically new meaning. My work was less about routine maintenance and more about the enrichment of each one's creativity and sense of self: less about playing a clerical role and more about human compassion and service.

As a priest, I now saw myself as a kind of midwife – a midwife of the sacredness already within the parishioners in the ordinariness of their days, and the truth of their relationships. Everything about them was grace-filled – when they encouraged each other, when they forgave each other, when they loved each other. This was God in action. I was the prism to help them perceive this, to see their true colours uniquely shining from the week-days of their lives.

The sacraments we celebrated in our parishes were

celebrations of the holiness already within our lives – in the joy of a new birth, in the pain of our darkness, in the holiness of human love, in the desires of our hearts, in reconciliation with the wider community, in the dream of the earth. Above all, the ever-deepening meanings of the Eucharist became the centre, the interpreter, the sustainer of our precarious and precious lives.

The new emphasis was on calling out the inner gifts of everyone, the encouraging of people to see themselves as made in God's image. We are God's delight. It was about helping people understand that the inner conversion of their hearts was what Jesus was after, not just the improved religious observance or increased church attendance that we often mistake for inner transformation.

This vision of God's reign among us increased our sensitivity to issues of justice everywhere, to the care of the earth, to engage with the destruction and exploitation caused by human greed. Parishioners were filled with a sense of their own responsibility for healing brokenness – within our communities and within our world. But first within their own hearts.

With minds, hearts and bodies we studied, worked and prayed. The inner journey preceded the outer one. We were often inspired by these words of our late Pope John Paul II. "What the world need now, are heralds of the Gospel, who are experts in humanity, familiar with their own emotions, able to share them with others, and who are at the same time, contemplatives who have fallen in love with God."

Around this time I also began to realise that "the faith" is caught, not just taught; that I myself have to be transformed before others will be. Only to the extent that I explore the inner complexity of my own heart will I ever be of any use to the people I serve. I have to learn how to know myself well because it is myself, with my sins and graces that comes across in my preaching, my serving, my leadership.

And the journey continues. Our ailing Church needs a new heart. My life is now devoted to deepening the awareness of this breathtaking vision, this spirituality of the heart, not only for the personal transformation of people's lives, but in the pastoral ministries of education, catechesis and preaching. During these final decades of my life, my ministry lies in speaking and writing on such vibrant issues.

Fr Daniel O'Leary is a priest of the Diocese of Leeds.

Being a Pygmy in Giant's Armour
The Petrine and Marian Principles

Mgr Mark O'Toole

It is common nowadays to talk of the priest as a relational being. One way of understanding this is through the universal call to holiness, particularly as it has been reflected on by the theologian Hans Urs von Balthasar.

Balthasar explores holiness in the Church through the Marian and Petrine Principles. Jesus Christ, when on earth, gathered around him a group of human individuals – Mary, Peter, the Apostles. We believe that the Risen Christ is present throughout history. Thus those who gathered around Jesus in the Gospels still continue to exist in some form now within the Church. Those chosen by the Lord represent a 'principle' of Church life, continuing the foundational experiences of those earliest believers. The most significant of these individuals are Mary and Peter.

The pastoral office given to Peter refers to the hierarchical and institutional dimension of the Church; this is the Petrine Principle. This dimension of Church life refers to the Apostolic Office and guarantees in the Church "objective holiness". I love the story told of Cardinal McCann, the former Archbishop of Cape Town. The doorbell rang and he went out to find two charismatic evangelists. "Good afternoon sir," one of them said, "have you received the Holy Spirit?" "Received the Holy Spirit?" said the Cardinal, "I give the Holy Spirit!"

Through the ministry entrusted to Peter and the apostles, the Holy Spirit comes to all God's people in Word, Sacrament and Magisterial Teaching. It means that when the sacraments are celebrated, and the Word proclaimed we can know that God is communicating His life to His people. This does not depend on the holiness of the individual priest, but is guaranteed by Christ in what he has handed on to Peter and the Apostles and those who participate in that ministry.

The Marian dimension manifests the response of human love to divine love. Mary's perfect "yes" of love to God meant that the mystery of Trinitarian life entered into history. Through Mary Christ became man, and the reality of the Church as the Body of Christ spread throughout space and time. The role of Mary then continues in the Church as the principle of personal holiness in the heart of each believer. Mary is the first of the disciples, not merely because she first responded to the gift of Christ, but also because it is under her that we are tutored in our discipleship of Christ. This is what is meant by the Marian Principle; the holiness born in the life of Mary is mirrored in the personal holiness of individual believers.

I remember hearing of a parish pilgrimage to Lourdes. You know what it looks like. There is the grotto with a statue of Our Lady in it. Above the grotto is the towering basilica Church. Catching her first glimpse of this, a young mother in the group sighed, "Oh, how beautiful. Look, Mary is holding up the Church."

Both Petrine and Marian Principles are essential dimensions of the life of the Church. In parish life one sees that it is the people who help us to discover what it means to be a priest. Ministerial priesthood cannot make sense without a baptised people whom it can serve; similarly the baptised need the ministerial priesthood if they are fully to manifest their high calling. One cannot exist without the other.

When we talk about the laity finding their rightful place I think it is really an invitation to try to rediscover a path of holiness in the life of each person and for the ordained ministry to try and serve that and call it forth. A Vatican document on Vocation (*In Verbo tuo*) speaks of the priest helping every baptised person to discover "the dream found in God's heart" because the person is found in the heart of God. Each priest is called to help people bring to fruition the dream that God has for them. Often, perhaps, it will make us realise that our people are infinitely more holy than we are.

I was Confessor to an enclosed community of nuns for about six years. One elderly sister came to Confession every week and just before she left the room, having received the words of absolution she would always say, "Thank you Fr Mark, for giving me the power of Christ". I used to feel about two inches tall. But that is the way it should be. Balthasar said that a priest is "a pygmy in giant's armour".

Participation in the Petrine Office is a grace to the whole Church but the lived holiness of our people is a grace and a consolation to those of us who are priests. Christ does not depend on our personal giftedness or holiness in order to give His life to His people. The Petrine Office has never for me meant some kind of "automatic grace" at work, but rather an acknowledgement of the vulnerability of the priest but an even greater affirmation of the faithfulness of God. God will continue to manifest in the Marian heart of his people the life of his beloved Son. Each priest has the tremendous privilege of participating in that ministry handed on to Peter and the Apostles. May we continue to be faithful in our ministry to that service to Mary and her lived holiness, which we so often see more readily in the lives of His people.

Mgr Mark O'Toole, Rector of Allen Hall Seminary, Chelsea, London.

The Priest is a Conduit

George Cardinal Pell

For Catholics, ministerial priests and the baptised are not in competition, much less conflict. They are complementary. Cardinal Newman said that the Church would look funny without the laity, but without the priests there would be no Church at all, only a gathering of Christians.

Every priest represents Christ, the head of the Church. Our Lord called priests to be shepherds of the flock, fishermen of souls. St Paul said that priests are ambassadors of Christ. All this remains true, even in an age of public clerical scandals. The treasure remains in the earthenware jar, even when the jar is cracked and filthy.

A priest's duties to his people are always the same and Isaiah spells them out: to tell the truth to the poor, to remind them of God's justice, to console the sad, to visit the imprisoned, to comfort the mourners and inspire hope in the downcast. All this is a tall order, but they are Christ's marching orders for us.

Our Lord is the greatest teacher in history, judged from the extent and longevity of his influence. His parables still haunt and disconcert us today. So too every priest must teach regularly what we have received from Christ and the apostles.

St Paul hammers this home to his unruly congregation in the port city of Corinth, without finesse and without too much imagination. The word of God is not to be watered down, as the truth is announced without shame or subterfuge. Such truths reveal the glory on the face of God, Paul claims, and the priest is at his best when he is simply a conduit, a conductor for God's power, when his weakness and his strengths do not impede the free flow of God's grace.

Usually this does not mean heroic self-sacrifice; no

melodrama, no abject humility, no dust and ashes, but regular service of those close to us, day in and day out. This is the true Christian alternative to pagan lordliness.

Naturally, our abilities as priests differ from area to area of Church life. Some are better community builders; others are instinctive consolers; some thrive on administration; others can teach and preach very easily. The list could go on.

However, there is another dimension to priestly life, which every priest can do well (because, we are told, God does most of the work) and that is to pray well and regularly for his people. It is probably the most important part of our work.

Western society is infecting our church, sapping our vitality. We are tempted to place the search for transcendence, the worship of mystery, on the margins; for those few so inclined. Being interested in God can become like music or ballet lessons for the children. More radically, others reduce God to an extension of the human person, the ground of our being.

All this means that the priest must also pray for himself, as regularly as he prays for his people, that his faith remains strong and a stimulus to hard work and initiative, not just an inert and receding backdrop. The priest needs to be regularly near God with his people in his heart. He will be able to help his people so much more if his prayer regularly takes him beyond his daily concerns.

Sometimes his prayer will be easy and beautiful, at other times it will be dry and distasteful, but prayer is founded in the daily round of small triumphs, routine and occasional disappointment. Prayer is not an extra, an embellishment; it is part of our work, part of our duty towards God and our people. In all things we must hold fast to prayer so that we may share with all mankind the word of God with joy.

George Cardinal Pell, Archbishop of Sydney.

Reflections on the Priesthood

Bishop Michael Putney

It was very obvious during the World Youth Day celebrations in Sydney that while young people were focused on Jesus Christ and the Eucharist, they also wanted to join in prayer with Pope Benedict XVI who represented for them the universal church to which they belonged.

As well, they were very enthusiastic if their own bishop was with them at any time, or if they saw him among the bishops from around the world. They were glad in a more intimate way if a priest from their home diocese was with them or crossed their paths.

The pope, their bishop and their priests were very tangible signs for them of their Catholic identity. This is not surprising. The identity of Catholics is built around Jesus Christ. He is present to them in the Word and in the sacraments, especially the Eucharist. But he is also present in a secondary way through those who are ordained to serve them as their pastors, and to preside at their celebrations of the Word of God and the Eucharist.

Ordination to priesthood establishes a unique relationship with Jesus Christ. He uses the one ordained as a way for himself to preside over the communion of those who have become one with him through baptism. This unique and indispensible role was taken for granted many decades ago in the West. It needs to be reclaimed today in our new context.

The Church has changed so that the unique role of the priest is not the only visible ministerial role in our parishes; and the world has changed so that Western culture has ceased to be supportive of religious faith and is sometimes opposed to it. The priest in the contemporary church and in a secular age has to know very clearly who he is and where he now fits in the church and the world if he is to make a difference, and even in some cases, to survive.

Despite the variety of ways in which people can now serve in the Church, the priest as a member of the church is alone ordained to preside over a community and its Eucharist, and to be a pastor for the whole community on behalf of Jesus Christ. This ministry has not ceased and must not be blurred. It is indispensible for the flourishing of the Church.

Priests no longer minister in isolation, but they alone have a ministry to everyone else in their church community. It is one of supporting, encouraging, educating, forming, governing, guiding, animating and leading as a true pastor. Presiding at the Eucharist and preaching remain the central expressions of this ministry because the Eucharist is the central expression of the life of everyone in the church.

The cultural context for this ministry is also very different because of our contemporary Western secular culture. This culture is not just something outside of the priest, it is also within himself and within his church community. At times it becomes much more powerful than the Catholic culture created by our faith.

Therefore, the priest has a particular role of carving out for everyone else and indeed for himself, an identity and a network of relationships that will shape our self-awareness more than the secular identity or network of relationships that also shapes our lives. People need to rediscover that they are Catholics before they are English, Australian, American or Irish. They are believers before they are anything else in life.

This is impossible without a deep experience of prayer. Only in prayer can we sink beneath the illusion that our secular culture offers us the way, the truth and the life. Only deep prayer gives rise to contemplation, which is seeing the whole of reality in terms of our relationship with God. This alone will make it possible for us to find his way, his truth and his life within our contemporary culture, which is to find Christ.

As pastors, priests need to be men who can share their faith and so can shape for themselves and others experiences of faith which are counter-cultural. Large gatherings like World Youth Day do this very well. But obviously the Church today needs other ways of networking that enable Catholics to belong consciously to a community or a body of human beings who are different from the "crowd" and to find their deepest sense of themselves within that body or community, and its celebration of the Eucharist.

This makes the role of the priest in our age very challenging but also very exciting. Jesus Christ calls priests to follow him not in the abstract, but in the concrete world and society in which they live. The gifts for ministry precisely for our culture and for our changing church were given to them for the asking through their ordination.

In this "Year of Priests", we could do nothing better than to re-discover these gifts and to use them with passion for the sake of our church.

Bishop Michael Putney, Bishop of Townsville, Australia.

Taking the First Step

Timothy Radcliffe OP

Although Jesus was never a member of the priestly caste, he is the model of priesthood and holiness of us all. I suggest to you that when Jesus speaks of himself as the Good Shepherd, "I have other sheep that are not of this fold", he is referring above all to our rootless, religiously parched friends and contemporaries – children of God, good people, but starved of the light of Christ in a brittle and neurotic secular world. To these people we, Christians of every denomination, are sent to bear witness to the light and the love of God. "Together and not in isolation" – that is the vocation and the strength of the ecumenical movement. That is the hope of which St Paul writes in his Letter to the Romans: "We who have the first fruits of the Spirit wait for adoption as sons... in this hope we are saved".

He embraces the untouchable, the lepers; he eats and drinks with sinners; he is the sacrificial lamb who dies on the altar of the cross. So the whole people of God is a holy and priestly people, because it embodies Christ's embrace of us all in our messy lives, with all their weakness and failures. The sacrament of that holiness is the Eucharist, in which Christ gave his body to us all, including the disciples who would betray and deny him. The holiness of the Church is shown in its inclusion of sinners, not their exclusion. As James Joyce would say of the Church, "Here comes everyone".

Let me make a confession. As the time for me to be ordained drew near, I began to have terrible doubts as to whether I was called to be a priest. I had become deeply repelled by clericalism, and by any hint of priestly superiority. I dreaded the hypocrisy of it, because I knew that I was no better than anyone else. I accepted ordination only in obedience to my brethren.

I finally came to love my priesthood in the confessional box. It was here that I discovered that ordination brings us close to people just when they feel farthest away from God. We are one with them, at their sides, as together we face human frailty, failure and sin, ours and theirs. I am suggesting that the ordained priest is called to embody in his life and being God's outreach to all of scattered humanity. This takes one beyond the dichotomy of those who see priesthood in terms of being and those who see it in terms of doing. All that we can do as ordained priests should express and embody the holiness of God's being in Christ, transforming the outsider into an insider, death into life, and sorrow into joy.

Our leadership is shown in being those who are prepared to take the first step: in reaching out to those who are excluded and marginalised, in offering and asking for forgiveness. In the parable of the prodigal son, reconciliation is achieved because both the younger son and the father take the first step in different ways. The son takes the first step in coming home, and when the father sees him in the distance, he takes the first step in going to meet him.

So for us to be leaders does not require that we be omni-competent, decisive people who tell everyone else what to do. It does require that we dare to take the first step in going before people, whether to welcome those who may not want us, to invite people to do more than they ever believed possible, to forgive and to ask for forgiveness. This can be lonely. True leadership, in this sense, can lead us to the solitude of the cross.

Perhaps in the universal ethos of the market, our leadership will be in daring to let fall the mask of competence, to face our own limitation and failure, and not be afraid of them. Leadership above all means taking the first step into vulnerability.

Timothy Radcliffe OP, former Master General of the Dominican Order.

Loudspeakers for Christ

Archbishop Gianfranco Ravasi

"Loudspeaker for Christ, not just with words but also by deeds." I vividly recall these words written in a biography to describe a priest who had rescued the writer from atheism. The image of the loudspeaker seems so modern, but behind it is the image of the "prophet", itself being a product of the Greek *phemi* (one who speaks) and *pro* (on behalf of). Prophets were not just spokespersons, but were ready to risk their very lives to proclaim the message entrusted to them, as any reader of Isaiah or Amos will remember. This is something we see in contemporary prophetic ministry too and in this context I think of the many priests whose work can be held up as an example.

Now that the Year for Priesthood is upon us, at the wish of Pope Benedict XVI, the entire ecclesial community has the opportunity to consider the figure of the priest in all its prophetic authenticity. Human, fragile, weak and even unfaithful, his is a necessary presence because he tells out permanently, by his being, the ever present Other. This puts into context what we take for granted, our daily lives and mundane concerns. As long as priests carry this message, giving and doing things in the name of Christ, then all worries about being marginalised and abandoned fall away.

One of Italy's more famous priests of the last generation, the educationalist Don Lorenzo Milani, wrote in his testimony, *Pastoral Experiences*, "Where is it written that priests have to make themselves loveable? Jesus did not achieve this, nor did he care to." This is a paradox but it contains more than a grain of truth. Our Lord was a sign of contradiction and had no hesitation in declaring that he brought a sword and would divide. His words leave no room for compromise, rather they penetrate consciences, separating the good and the bad, truth and lies, love and egoism.

Another Catholic writer, the Frenchman Georges Bernanos, in his *La grande peur des bien-pensants,* noted that "one of the main culprits, the only culprit perhaps, of the poisoning of souls is the mediocre priest." We can be tried under this charge when we are no longer "transparent", letting the light of the Word and witness of Christ speak through us. So too can the laity when this voice and light become inaudible and invisible, disappearing into the texture of society, colourless and bland.

But let us not forget that Jesus loved and was loved by his disciples, by the women who followed him and by the crowds too. He was fond of friendship and showed mercy and attention to the poor and lowly: "Come to me, you who are tired and oppressed and I will give you rest ... I am meek and humble of heart." What we priests receive today in affection and nearness when followed by crowds is something we can offer up in thanks for the many priests and prophets who have preceded us in the priesthood of Jesus Christ, whose glory we proclaim from the rooftops.

Archbishop Gianfranco Ravasi, President of the Pontifical Council for Culture.

Leaving Safe Harbours
– or –
On Board the Titanic?

Fr Bill Redmond

The librettist of the popular Gilbert and Sullivan operettas always gave his works two titles, for example, "HMS Pinafore" or "The Lass that loved a Sailor". Gilbert's point was to explain the first (short) title by the second (longer) one. His tale here is about a humble Able Seaman who falls in love with a wealthy Captain's daughter.

Now take the two titles for this little article. The second is a wee bit longer than the first. But more to the point – does the second *explain* the first? Is the "Leaving Safe Harbours" just a dumbed-down way of saying that we're aboard the ill-fated Titanic, out in mid-Atlantic, and about to be holed by an enormous and lethal iceberg? (And we've no Leonardo di Caprio or Kate Winslett aboard to improve the view!) The answer to that lies entirely in how we, as clergy and laity, respond to the quite radical changes that the "Leaving Safe Harbours" process is urging upon us.

Some facts: fewer clergy, mainly middle-aged-plus, some in indifferent health; far fewer weekend Mass attenders, some middle-aged, many elderly, very few under 35; "loadza" churches, many in the wrong places and in the main half-empty, weekend by weekend. For some, let's be honest, this is where the great liner – thought to be "unsinkable" – meets her doom. All these Cassandras are about to be proved right. "Save us Lord, we're going down!"

Or are we? Some more facts, perhaps. Western society is ageing, so inevitably is the European Church; smaller congregations now assemble, but IN SPITE OF, not BECAUSE OF, family/social pressure; we have too many church buildings because in the late '50s too many were built – and arguably for the wrong reasons. But, above all, two facts stand out:

> 1. When thick on the ground, the clergy took too much on themselves; now, diminished in numbers, we must re-focus our efforts towards basic evangelisation and the dignified celebration of the Mass and Sacraments.

> 2. Cardinal Hume led us into the 'Age of the Laity'. This present period of evolution challenges the Baptised Lay Faithful to fulfil their roles as Prophet, Priest and King in the Church.

"On board the Titanic"? Only if we panic or (worse) dig our heels in and refuse to adapt to a new ideal of Communion where "Father" does less, but better; and the lay faithful continue to do more, in the superb way they are already doing so much. If I may dare correct Archbishop Kelly of Liverpool, we're not leaving safe harbours – we left them a decade or so ago! However, our first "model" of change – "clustering" – has not really proved a success. The "Leaving Safe Harbours" model of a Community gathered around the human sign of three or four priests who support one another in their ministry is an alternative that we must be bold enough to try.

Not the Titanic. But not a cruise on the QE II either! Rather an honest and sincere effort by all of us to row TOGETHER in the same boat. We'll be sweating so hard we'll melt the infamous iceberg!

Fr Bill Redmond, Parish Priest of Our Lady of Perpetual Succour, Widnes, Archdiocese of Liverpool.

A Young Priest
Begins a Journey of Love

Fr David Reilly

When a priest celebrates his First Mass it is traditional to ask another priest to preach the homily but at my own First Mass in November 2008 I decided to preach myself. After over six years of formation I thought it best to get on with the job! The Mass was on the Feast of Christ the King, and the Gospel was the parable of the Last Judgement. This was a brilliant Gospel to hear on the first day of priesthood: Christ, the Shepherd-King, teaching us how to serve and love others.

A key element in preparing that significant homily was reflecting on my formation and preparation for ordination. I would like to share some of those thoughts and prayers here. In a sense, they have accompanied me during these first months of priesthood. It is a reflection on the priesthood and love. The critical question for me has been: how can a priest learn to have the heart of a "good shepherd" like Jesus Christ?

I was very much aware of a paragraph from the Second Vatican Council's Decree on Priests which is striking in its lucidity: "Priests should remember that in performing their tasks they are never alone. Relying on the power of Almighty God and believing in Christ who called them to share in his priesthood, they should devote themselves to their ministry with complete trust, knowing that God can intensify in them the ability to love." (*Presbyterorum Ordinis, 22*). For me, that is a wonderful exhortation for priests today. We are asked to open ourselves up, to abandon our fears, so that God can intensify in us the "ability to love". God has given us so much love; these words urge us to allow God's love to grow deeper, so that it will become the source of our ministry. Pope Benedict wrote, "Anyone who wishes to give love must also receive love as a gift … to become such a source, one must drink constantly anew from the original source." (*Deus Caritas Est, 7*) We rightly talk about priesthood in terms of service, but not so often in terms of love. That is surprising because Jesus spoke of his own life and sacrifice in terms of love when he said, 'Greater love has no man than this, that a man lay down his life for his friends.' (Jn 15:13).

The priestly formation that we receive today is now largely inspired by the beautiful document *Pastores Dabo Vobis*. That exhortation was particularly creative in that it did not focus primarily on the rights and duties of the priest, as had happened in the past, but spoke refreshingly of pastoral charity as the binding force uniting a priest's life, mission and spirituality. Pastoral charity is essentially the "gift of self", of one's life to the Church, to prayer, to the liturgy and to the various pastoral activities that are part of a priest's life. As a student, this helped me to make sense of the sometimes disparate elements of pastoral work. We priests know firsthand the richness of our ministry on any given day: baptising, teaching, marrying, anointing; but with the busy nature of our ministry there is a danger that these different moments become detached, staccato elements in a fraught existence. I want to keep a sense that through prayer, especially the Eucharist, Christ's love will feed us, so that pastoral charity will connect these, making my priesthood whole and united in Christ.

In his book *In the Name of Jesus*, Henri Nouwen reflects on what qualities are important for future ministry. He says the decisive question asked by Jesus of Peter was not to do with how successful Peter might be, but was, "Do you love me?" I often reflect on that. Already there are times when I feel far from successful, when I worry about the way I have dealt with something, or worry about my ability. Each day, I need to ask myself anew: how can a priest learn to have the heart of a good shepherd? How can I renew the gift of self, and how can I let God intensify in me the ability to love?

Fr David Reilly, assistant priest of St Patrick's Wapping.

At the time of going to print he is the most recently ordained priest in the Archdiocese of Westminster and is also, at 30 years, the youngest in age.

Significant Steps

Bishop Arthur Roche

The journey towards priesthood is marked by significant stages. Each stage brings with it new duties, new responsibilities and new challenges; each stage marking a deeper call in our relationship and commitment to Christ, illustrating a deeper personal involvement in his Paschal Mystery, which is at the very heart of what it is to be a priest.

The Church takes great care that those who are called to the office of priest should be deeply involved in every aspect of this mystery through the celebration of the Word, the celebration of the Sacraments and, because this is a demanding way of life, through a personal and joyful response to an invitation from Christ to his closest collaborators – an invitation to self-emptying.

The Lectorate, for example, not only invites the candidate to proclaim and teach with greater care and skill from the Sacred Scriptures, but to make those very writings the daily, indispensable foundation on which to build his own life. It is a commission, but it is also a challenge. If we take the Church's call seriously then our lives will change and in turn we will, from minds and hearts that are themselves daily converted, authentically break for others the word of God. This personal commitment to God's word helps us to fix our eyes upon a greater reality and to see the things around us with a wisdom that alone comes from God. We are to be, in the words of the prophet Malachi, *messengers sent by the Lord, to prepare a way before him* (Mal 3:1) – men who have been chosen to share with others those things which were prepared by God's providence for all the nations to see – a light that enlightens and gives glory to God through the ministry of the Church.

The call to be an Acolyte is also an important stage

of involvement in the Paschal Mystery. The Greek word, ακολοθεω, means "to follow God" more closely. Why? Because communion, unity, is at the heart of God's own existence. An Acolyte is a Minister of Communion. At this stage, the Church is stressing the centrality of the Eucharist in the life of a priest. But lest he should get the wrong end of the stick, the Church makes it very clear that, together with the privilege of carrying the Blessed Sacrament to others, comes also the responsibility of entering into communion, of "being in union with", not only Christ but also the very people whom he has been called to serve. The Church is inviting the Acolyte to be a builder and a constructor in a world that is divided and which is often disposed to a spirit of negativity and destruction at many levels. There is no room here for a purveyor of cynicism – our eyes and our way of life have to be focussed and built on greater realities. The lesson to be learnt at this stage is to act as a co-responsible worker in the mission of Christ, to encourage the return to unity of the scattered flock, not only outside our community but also within it.

Then there is Candidacy which has its own special part to play at the very heart of the Paschal Mystery. At this stage, the Church is looking for a personal and public response as to whether the candidate wishes to enter, even more profoundly through his own self-emptying, into the mystery of Christ who gave up His own life for the sake of His brothers and sisters. This commitment, of course, is not just a matter of personal preference. It is a response to an invitation from the Church, backed up by those responsible for assessing the candidate's suitability, to commit himself to live in a priestly way – to dispose himself, in this period of engagement, as it were, to greater consideration of three elements that are at the heart of Christ's priestly response to the Father: of being attentive to someone greater than oneself, of being completely available for the mission while entering, at the same time, into a strong and loving relationship with God and the whole Church.

The first element has to do with the will of God exercised through the promise of obedience – of listening attentively to the teachings of the Church, and living according to those teachings; by responding willingly and lovingly and respectfully to the bishop and to those to whom he gives authority. In saying *yes* to the promise of obedience, he is saying to God that he wishes to fulfil the Father's will rather than his own designs, and to establish His Kingdom rather than build his own. Like Christ he is invited to put aside any consideration of status and will join the countless ranks of priests who, throughout the ages, have served the Lord in freedom and witnessed to the world that the law of God is more important than any human law or personal preference.

The second element of Christ's relationship of complete, unimpeded openness to the Father is to be found in His celibate life. In saying *yes* to Christ, the candidate will be saying *yes* to a life of consecrated and chaste celibacy that denies him the right to a wife and a family. In this way, the Lord asks him to be a signpost to the Church, to bear witness before the whole world to the fact that it is possible to love God alone and that He should be loved above all things. People may ridicule this choice, call it a waste of a life, but his choice will speak loudly about his belief that God is at the centre of his heart and that all he does and says springs from a profound love of Him. It speaks of the power of God shining through our human weakness (cf. Preface for Martyrs). As St Paul reminds us: *Glory be to him whose power, working in us, can do infinitely more than we can ask or imagine* (Eph 3:20). This power to love comes from God and not from us. A celibate life is a great treasure for it shows us that the future priest is willing to stake his life on God as a reality. It is his road to God and his greatest freedom for him and for others.

Finally, like Christ, he will be asked to take to his heart the people and the concerns of the Church and the world in which we live – to go early in the morning and late at night to a lonely place to be with the Father. To say *yes* to a life of prayer is to say yes to a life of praise and worship – spending time giving glory to God out of sheer love, relying on His power working through *our human weakness*. The special care of the candidate, indeed that of all bishops, priests and deacons, is to take to his heart, and place before the Lord, everyone who in this topsy-turvey world of ours is in need, and to pray on behalf of those who cannot pray for themselves. Here he will gain his own strength, too, and develop the eyes and the ears, the words and the healing touch of God Himself.

These stages along the path to priesthood are steps towards generous living and dedicated commitment. They are signs of a burning desire to live closely to the Lord in His own life, sufferings, death and resurrection – in other words, every aspect of the Paschal Mystery. They serve as *a lamp for our steps and a light for our paths*, (Ps 119:105) not only for the candidate for priesthood but also for the whole Church.

Bishop Arthur Roche, Bishop of Leeds.

The Source of Our Joy

Mgr Stephen Rossetti

More than a few of the laity visualise priesthood as a rather dour, sombre life. They equate it with many sacrifices and few joys. Of course, there are some real sacrifices. One immediately thinks of the celibate's lack of a spouse, children, and a home. Thus, there is a popular conception that he is living a sad life. But nothing could be further from the truth.

Jesus made us a promise: "And everyone who has given up houses or brothers or sisters or father or mother or children or lands for the sake of my name will receive a hundred times more, and will inherit eternal life" (NAB Mt 19:29). Jesus clearly implies that this overflowing blessing is given to us even now.

Have priests truly received the one-hundred-fold blessing of the Lord? Jesus promised us his gifts of joy and peace: "That my joy might be in you and your joy might be complete" (Jn 15:11) and again, "Peace I leave with you; my peace I give to you" (Jn 14:27). If God has blessed us priests, it must include these central gifts of Jesus – joy and peace. Are priests really happy people?

The answer will be personal for every priest. Each of us receives, in the measure we are able, the gifts the Lord offers. There are indeed a few priests who are individually unhappy. But as a whole, can one say that the priesthood has received these gifts? Are priests, as a group, a happy lot?

The best way to answer the question is to ask the priests themselves. In 2003 I conducted a survey of diocesan and religious priests in the United States. Of those who responded (64.9 percent), over 80 percent said their morale was good or very good. Over 90 percent agreed with the statement: "Overall, I am happy as a priest". I am currently conducting a follow-up study, which is beginning to show similar results, indicating that priests are a very happy and satisfied group.

Why? What is the source of their joy? There are likely to be many reasons. Even though priests give up having their own families, they are surrounded by people who love and support them. Priests consistently say that parishioners warmly invite them into their homes and into their lives. Priests give up having their own family, but inherit many more. Jesus promised that they would; he said they would receive one hundred times as many.

But there are other reasons for the exceptionally high levels of happiness in priesthood. In *Gaudete in Domino*, Pope Paul VI spoke to us about the great need for joy in our hearts, the terrible lack of it today, and the source of true joy. He wrote:

> "But it is necessary here below to understand properly the secret of the unfathomable joy which dwells in Jesus and which is special to Him… If Jesus radiates such peace, such assurance, such happiness, such availability, it is by reason of the inexpressible love by which He knows that He is loved by His Father."

Succinctly put, Jesus' joy, which he shares with us, finds its source in his awareness of the unsurpassable love of the Father for him.

This is true of our lives as well. I have worked for over sixteen years with priests and religious who are suffering from psychological and spiritual difficulties. Time and again, I have witnessed the tremendous healing that takes place when God's love touches their hearts directly.

Oftentimes, these suffering people will come to our centre with an intellectual idea that God loves them, but not truly feeling nor having experienced it themselves. During their recovery programme, it is not uncommon that they will have a significant spiritual experience in which they actually feel that God loves them personally and totally, just as they are. When this happens, the transformation is profound.

There are many sources of joy in a priest's life. But the most important is his spiritual connection with our loving Father. Like Jesus, when we truly know, in the deepest recesses of our hearts, that we are loved unconditionally by the Father, we are filled with an eternal joy.

A priestly life is a life of joy. Of course, this joy does not erase the reality of the Cross in a priest's life any more than it erased the Cross in Jesus' life. But our joy is a gift from God who showers his love and joy on us in abundance. In this life, we receive one hundred fold, and in the next life, we will see the Source of our joy with unfettered eyes.

Mgr Stephen J. Rossetti, priest of the Diocese of Syracuse, New York and the President and CEO of Saint Luke Institute in Silver Spring, Maryland.

A Call for Vocations

Archbishop Faustino Sainz Muñoz

We thank Almighty God for those who have gone before us and transmitted the faith of the Apostles to us, especially for those who have been members of this parish, perhaps even our own families, relatives and friends. We remember also the responsibility that is now given by the Lord to us. He asks us to be His witnesses for the future and faithfully to hand on that which has been entrusted to us, in all its fullness, the Faith of the Church, not just those elements which are popular in the culture of our day.

Today, I wish to ask a favour, which will also help to ensure that St Mary's can continue with shepherds into the future. Pray please, for good and generous Catholic families, for it is within our Catholic families that we first learn how to pray, to have quiet time, and how to serve and begin to discover to what it is that God is calling us, whether marriage and parenthood, religious life or priesthood or the single life. I know that in this parish there are many good and "productive" families, from which vocations for priesthood or for consecrated life would be possible.

Allow me to tell you a little about my personal experience. I must tell you that I am the second of ten children and I remember that at the end of my University studies I was rather apprehensive about telling my father that I hoped to go to the seminary because I thought that he might want me to help him in supporting my younger brothers and sisters. When I spoke to him he surprised me with his reaction. He said to me: "God has always taken care of our family and I am sure he will continue to do so. What you don't know is that since your mother and I have been married, each day we have prayed that one of our sons should be called to the priesthood. So be calm and have no fear in following God's call."

I must say that, when my family prayed the Rosary at home, we knew that one of the intentions for which we prayed was "Vocations", but my parents never told us that it was their desire that one of us should be called to the priesthood!

As the Holy Father reminded us during his visit to Valencia: "The family is a necessary good for peoples, an indispensable foundation for society and a great and lifelong treasure for couples. It is a unique good for children, who are meant to be the fruit of the love, of the total and generous self-giving of their parents. To proclaim the whole truth about the family, based on marriage as a domestic Church and a sanctuary of life, is a great responsibility incumbent upon all."

Good families produce good priests and religious sisters. Good priests and religious support and sustain good and generous family life. So pray, please, for all our Catholic families, including your own, that they may be open to the call of God, made to each unique individual.

Archbishop Faustino Sainz Muñoz, Apostolic Nuncio to Great Britain.

From a sermon preached at St Mary's Holly Place, Hampstead, London in 2006.

Thoughts on Priestly Ministry Based on the Hospitality of Abraham

Christoph Cardinal Schönborn OP

Genesis tells in a striking way of God's visit to Abraham (Gen 18:16-33). Abraham welcomed the mysterious travellers to his tent by the oak of Mamre. He became a friend of God because he practised hospitality and thereby entertained God. Priestly ministry shows often and in many ways that love of God and love of neighbour are inseparable. This hospitality towards the travellers reveals itself as hospitality towards God. The Letter to the Hebrews echoes this scene: those that have shown hospitality have also taken in angels (Heb 13:2). These three figures are angels, messengers of God, and at the same time God himself is in these messengers. He who practises hospitality opens his heart and door to God. Conversely, he who opens his heart to God, cannot close it to his neighbour.

Secondly, Abraham has an immediate experience of God. "He saw three and worshipped one", St Augustine said, "*tres vidit et unum adoravit*". He sees three angels but addresses them as "my Lord". In these three messengers, Abraham encounters in a mysterious way the one and triune God. And so we have before us the icon of the Trinity of the Eastern Church, showing the three angels as Abraham's guests, representing the one and triune God. The encounter with the living God is the centre of the priestly way and life.

Thirdly, Abraham becomes the great intercessor. Most impressively he bargains with God, one could almost say he argues, wrestles to save sinful mankind. The just man cannot tolerate injustice. And so Abraham argues with God: You cannot destroy the just together with the unjust. In his passion for God's justice, which has the welfare of humanity at heart, he bargains with God who agrees: "If

I find ten who are righteous, I shall not destroy Sodom and Gomorrah". He brings his fervent intercession to God because it is God's dearest wish not to lose one person. And so it is also the duty of the priest to intercede earnestly for mankind so as not to lose even one.

This leads us to the final and most profound mystery of priesthood: Abraham stopped at ten. Only one is righteous. For his sake all will be saved. Jesus Christ is the righteous one. If we are allowed to perform priestly ministry, this we do as servants of the One, who made many righteous through his dedication, his self-sacrifice and his resurrection. This is what we celebrate in the Eucharist, Christ's sacrifice, so that not one is lost. Thus God's justice shows itself as merciful, God gives life to all.

Christoph Cardinal Schönborn OP, Archbishop of Vienna.

Being a Priest is about Serving Amazing People

Fr Peter-Michael Scott

Sarah was eight years old and dying of leukaemia. Understandably her mother and father were distraught. Every day or two I used to visit the children's ward and chat with Sarah and her parents. Sarah could not comprehend she would die, but did understand that she would have a funeral. After she had received communion, she used to prop herself up on her elbows and talk to me. "It has to be pink" she would say. "Like a Barbie funeral!" "What about me?" I would ask. "Do I have to wear pink?" "Well, it would be good if you could", she said. "Have you a pink vestment thingy you can wear?"

Sarah's mum and dad could not cope with the pink funeral conversation and would try and sidetrack her by promising her a "Ken and Barbie" private jet, complete with matching pink and blue parachutes. One day, after another conversation about pink funerals – which was expertly side-stepped by talk of a Ken and Barbie private jet – Sarah asked her parents if the promised aeroplane could take the two glamorous action figures to the moon. "If that's what you want it to do… it will do it" replied her mum.

Sarah's parents were very kind and always greeted me with a hug. Before visiting her I would chat to one or both of them about how they were coping. They would honestly say that they could not utter the words "Sarah is dying". This vivacious, intelligent girl was their only child, they loved her, and could not comprehend what life would be like without her. I would sit and listen, drink cup after cup of tea and offer box after box of tissues.

After my visit I would go back to the hospital chapel, kneel and pray that somehow Sarah and her parents

181

would come to some shared acceptance of her imminent death.

One evening, when it was dark, Sarah asked her mother if the nurse would telephone me. My pager sounded and I was summoned to the children's ward.

When I arrived on the ward, Sarah was sitting on her bed wrapped in her favourite pink blanket and attached to a drip stand (her "Ken" she called it). "Can you come outside with me and Mum and Dad?" she asked.

I looked at her parents and her mother said. "She wants to go outside and tell us something. She will not go, unless you come." As she said this her mother reached down and stroked her daughter's pale hairless head.

We went outside. Sarah was carried by her dad, and a nurse steered her drip stand. It was a mild starry night and the moon was full. We sat on a bench. Sarah sat on her dad's knee. After a moment of stillness, Sarah said, "Mum and Dad, I know you don't want me to die, but I will."

She stopped speaking for a fraction of a second and then pointed at the full moon. "Tonight you can see the moon, but in the morning it will be gone, but you know you will see it again. In the same way, I will die, go to Jesus, and you will not see me ... but like the moon, you can be certain that eventually you will see me again."

We all sat stunned.

"I want to go back to the ward now", she said and relaxed into her father's arms.

Two nights later, Sarah died peacefully at home dressed in pink, with her mum and dad at her side.

Fr Peter-Michael Scott, Archbishop of Westminster's Advisor for Healthcare Chaplaincy.

An Archbishop's Call to Service

Archbishop Peter Smith

Christ has given us the great gift of the sacraments for our nourishment and healing. He gives us too the gift of personal prayer to draw us into a deeper personal relationship with him. And it is within this community of faith that we are all helped by each other's example to grow in love and in humble service of others, especially those in need. Along with the sacraments and personal prayer, we need the encouragement and support of each other, if we are to take seriously, and fulfil, the mission he has given to us to "proclaim the gospel to all peoples."

This "communion" of all the baptised, the Church, has been established by Christ as a priestly people, in which we all share in different degrees in the one priesthood of Christ. As it is expressed in the Preface of today's Mass, "God planned that this one priesthood should continue in his Church. To the people he has made his own through baptism and the anointing of the Holy Spirit, Jesus Christ gives a share of this royal priesthood. And from this royal priesthood of all the baptised, Christ freely chooses some men to share his sacred ministry through the laying on of hands, the prayer of consecration and the outpouring of the same Spirit." So those of us who are ordained and anointed with the Holy Spirit have our "mission" too, specifically within the body of the Church.

As ordained priests we are called to be the shepherds of the Church, following the model and example of Christ the Good Shepherd. Our task is to gather and to lead. Our task is to nourish God's people by word and sacrament, to serve through dedicated pastoral care, to recognise and promote the proper mission of the laity within the Church, and particularly within the world. Within these fragile vessels is a great treasure given by God through Jesus

Christ. It is a great gift, but it is also a great responsibility. Over the centuries the People of God have not ceased to put their trust in the power of Christ at work through the ministry of priests and bishops through the ages, despite at times our evident weakness and fragility.

Those of us who are ordained must never forget that the good that we do comes not so much from ourselves but flows from the gift of God's grace. The authority and power given to us through the laying on of hands and the gift of the Holy Spirit is always and only to be used in the service of God's people. Our calling is not to domination, not to lording it over others. It is a call to humble service after the example of the Good Shepherd. "I came not to be served, but to serve and to give my life as a ransom for many." We too, as disciples, are called to follow Jesus on the way of the cross. But in following humbly and generously the way of the Lord, we do so specifically in representing to his Church, his flock, the person of Jesus Christ as Head and Shepherd.

So let's all give thanks today to the God who has given us his only Son to be our Way, our Truth and our Life, and who has blessed us in so many ways; to God who has given us the gift of each other in all our uniqueness and variety, in all our strengths and weaknesses, in all our joys and sorrows. We ask him to give us the grace and strength to continue our journey together, strengthened by the grace of the sacraments, firm in faith, filled with hope and empowered by that divine love to follow wherever he may lead us.

Archbishop Peter Smith, Archbishop of Cardiff.
Address given at the Mass of Chrism, 2009.

Out of Darkness into Light

Bishop George Stack

Our religion is not merely a spiritual reality or a religion of words alone. It is a religion of signs and symbols and sacraments. The sacred actions we undertake in our worship make real the events which they signify. This is because we are drawn into union with God through the human and divine action of Jesus Christ in the atoning sacrifice which he offers for all people. He is the one priest who brings us into union with God through his death on the cross in obedience and in love – for God and for the whole of humanity.

It is through this communion that those who believe are baptised into the life, death and resurrection of Jesus. They are empowered to worship God not in merely human ways, but in God's own way. Self sacrificing love is the sign of God's activity on our behalf. That is why the Church calls its members a "Priestly People". United with Jesus we are able to offer praise and honour to God "Through Him, with Him, in Him, in the Unity of the Holy Spirit" by which "all honour and Glory are Yours for ever and ever. Amen."

The decree *Lumen Gentium* of the Second Vatican Council described the "priesthood of the laity" in the following words. "The baptised, by regeneration and the anointing of the Holy Spirit, are consecrated as a spiritual house and a holy priesthood, in order that through all these works which are those of the Christian man, they may offer spiritual sacrifices and proclaim the perfection of Him who has called them out of darkness into His own marvellous light." (*LG*, 10) (cf. 1 Pet 2:4-10).

But what of those ordained into the ministerial priesthood? *Lumen Gentium* goes on to say "Though they differ essentially, and not only in degree, the common

185

priesthood of the faithful and the ministerial priesthood are none the less ordered to one another; each in its own proper way shares the priesthood of Christ" (*LG*, 10).

Put briefly, those who are ordained priests dedicate their lives to enabling the priestly people to worship God in spirit and in truth. Their service and dedication is expressed in terms of the "headship" of the Body of Christ in a particular time and place and community. The priest is head of the worshipping community not to inhibit or dominate or distort but in order to animate it, inspire it and enable it to become what it is called to be.

One of the many awe inspiring actions performed by the Bishop at the ordination of a priest is the *Traditio Instrumentorum*, the handing over of the symbols of office to the newly ordained. The paten with the bread and the chalice containing the wine are the symbols of everything the priest is called to do and to be. The words spoken at that moment are both a comfort and a challenge for the one who is to exercise this office in and for the Church: "Accept the gifts of the people to be offered to God. Be conscious of what you are doing. Be as holy as the actions you perform. Model your life after the mystery of the Lord's cross."

The cross remains at the crossroads of human existence. It is the place where every person has to face all that would cause us to say that God is not present in the midst of human difficulty, human suffering, and even sin, offering forgiveness, healing and reconciliation. Cardinal Basil Hume spoke often to priests on the place of suffering, the place of the cross, in our lives. His words continue to make a profound impact on me and the way I conduct my priestly life:

> "If you have never been through darkness, then you simply cannot speak to people about the light. If you have never been through doubt you probably cannot speak eloquently about faith. You have to know about that side of life – the crucifixion side,

the passion side – in order to be able to speak about the Resurrection side."

Jesus embraced all these things on the cross. That is why he says to his priests "Do this in remembrance of me."

Bishop George Stack, Auxiliary Bishop of Westminster.

The Priest in the Parish

Mgr Tom Stack

An average parish congregation offers a human spectrum which represents different degrees of belonging to the parish community. This will range from the securely committed, mostly elderly, to the more ambivalent, mostly younger, who may be hanging in to worship by the proverbial "skin of their teeth" and for whom church-going, either regular or periodic is no longer perceived as obligatory. Their connection with the church may be sustained by a thread of sentiment, a residual loyalty, or support for their children who challenge them by relaying religious lore from school to home. But there is also another category to be found in the religious spectrum; a core of reflective adults, well educated and theologically alive, who cherish Christian life but are increasingly demanding in their expectations in terms of liturgy and broader parish ministry.

So much for the make up of the modern parish. How does the priest see the parish and his ministry within it? He is aware of how priestly ministry has been designed and has worked historically, corresponding as it has to varying models of church in different eras. He understands that the contemporary world, which he inhabits, sets the agenda for his pastoral endeavours. He is practical and "existentialist"; embracing the reality of his milieu as he finds it and not as he might wish it to be. He construes every individual person as a free and responsible agent, determining his or her own spiritual development. He knows, moreover, that the existence of God is never so clear that belief is inevitable, or ever so obscure that belief is impossible. No matter how remote from explicit gospel concerns the preoccupations of people in general may be, he suspects that there is a large measure of truth in the adage that "all questions are ultimately theological". In spite of the blurring of spiritual priorities which temporal and occupational anxieties may bring, the pastor recognises that the fundamental quest for meaning and values is never too far below the surface of human lives. The instinct that edges all towards relationships of one kind or another hints at the importance of community, however obscurely this may be divined. This in turn poses questions concerning the ultimate source of living and loving. In the phrase of the Irish poet Brendan Kennelly: "Self knows that self is not enough".

First and foremost, the very presence of the priest in the community will be referential; pointing towards the domain of the spirit wherein the presence of God may be disclosed. He is a sign of an order other than of the everyday. His position is that of an interrogative figure, symbolically posing questions that transcend mortgages, supermarkets and school runs. If that sounds like a pretentious claim, it may be moderated by two considerations. First, the priest's witness and work is not to be seen as conferring spiritual gifts and perspective on members of the community. Where the baptised are concerned, his function is rather to affirm a faith that is already theirs and help to elicit a response to what is a prior endowment; their own graced capacity to develop and enhance their knowledge and love of God. This gift and destiny is antecedent to any priestly ministry. Secondly, the priest understands his ministry as a service rather than a status; who he is, being subordinated to what he does. He is called to stimulate and encourage all by every means towards the fulfilment of the Pauline prayer:

> May he give you the power through his Spirit for your hidden self to grow strong, so that Christ may live in your hearts through faith, and then, planted in love and built on love, you will with all the saints have strength to grasp the breadth and the length, the height and the depth; until, knowing the love of

Christ, which is beyond all knowledge, you are filled with the utter fullness of God.

(Eph 3:16-19)

It is a truism that the individual priest, in terms of temperament and talent, will always be limited in his pastoral capacity. His fundamental purpose is to try to build up the believing community entrusted to his care. He is not primarily a "cultic" figure but an evangelist. The word he preaches is not his own but the Word of God. As a community leader, he begins by understanding that his first witness to the ideal of community is to promote and be seen to promote fellowship with other priests with whom he works in the parish. The fraternal relationship which exists between priests themselves will be a distinct example to the wider community.

One obvious form of pastoral limitation is that a priest, no matter how gifted, can never be equally competent as preacher, liturgist, administrator, counsellor, youth mentor and fundraiser. It is clearly unrealistic that his job description traditionally casts him as an omni-competent figure. However, the difficulties and limitations of ministry are largely offset by the widespread goodwill that still exists towards priests in parishes. Even when religious practise is in decline priests will rarely be received other than courteously in the homes of parishioners. Their role as spiritual agents in the community is largely accepted as retaining a corporate relevance and the question of priestly identity in the beginning of this century is on balance more academic than real. Residents in a parish may not always respond positively to the church's mission and ministry but they still know what it is about; notwithstanding the possibility that this recognition of the priestly role may itself become a launching pad for dissent or even its dismissal.

The Church in miniature exists in each parish the world over. This means that the fullness of Christian life exists in every single Christian community. The late

190

speaker of the U.S. Congress, Tipp O'Neill, once famously remarked that "all politics is local". In a sense we can say that all church is local, although linked of course to a wider and larger community. The Church as well as being a visible, social, entity is also constituted by an inner spiritual life which we speak of as "Spirit-filled" or the "Body of Christ". What is true of the church in its geographical and historical entity is likewise true of what we call a parish.

Catholic parishioners were accustomed to interpreting their role as that of helping the priest to do his work. Nowadays, this order may be reversed; the priest's function becoming that of helping the community of ministries to fulfil their true pastoral entitlement. This exciting pastoral inversion suggests an ecclesiastical equivalent of a Copernican Revolution! A more sober formulation of this might be that all members of the parish, including the priest, join in tending their graced project of building a family of faith, hope and love.

Mgr Tom Stack is a priest of the Archdiocese of Dublin and Pastor Emeritus of Milltown Parish.

The Joy of Commitment

Mgr Roderick Strange

Did Jesus ever tell a lie? We may recoil piously from the very idea, but if pressed to offer an example, we might choose the words we find in St Matthew's Gospel for the feast of the Sacred Heart: "My yoke is easy and my burden is light" (Mt 11:27). No, it isn't, we might protest; your yoke is hard and your burden heavy. But, when challenged, I imagine Jesus would hold his ground: my yoke is easy and my burden is light, he would insist, when you take them up without reserve. We are called to commitment.

When I was a boy, I often went with my father to watch a rugby match on Saturday afternoons. On one occasion, after a fierce tackle, a player came off injured. 'What's happened?' I said. "Looks like a broken collarbone", my father answered. "Did he hit him too hard?" I asked, thinking of the impact of the tackle. "No," Dad replied, "not hard enough." We get hurt when we are half-hearted, not when we are fully committed.

The feast of the Sacred Heart, the opening day of this Year of the Priesthood, is a natural day for celebrating the commitment that is integral to ordained ministry, for it celebrates Jesus' commitment to us, that love without limit that was revealed supremely by his death on the cross. The true statue of the Sacred Heart, we should always remind ourselves, is not the figure with the neatly trimmed beard and moustache, swathed in white and red, with a heart improbably visible on his robe, but the man nailed to the tree. If we are to realise what commitment entails, we must look to the cross, contemplate the crucified.

There are many ways of doing that. One of them is to ponder the words he spoke when crucified. They are utterly familiar, but people often fail to notice that they appear in different Gospels. So it is only in the earliest

Passion tradition, represented by Mark and Matthew, that Jesus cries out in agony, "My God, my God, why have you forsaken me?" (Mk 15:34; Mt 27:46). Luke alone, writing later, contains those three words, one filled with pardon: "Father, forgive them, for they do not know what they are doing" (Lk 23:34); another with compassion: "Truly, I tell you, today you will be with me in Paradise" (Lk 23:43); and the third revealing self-sacrifice: "Father, into your hands I commend my spirit" (Lk 23:46). And only in John's Gospel do we hear the words of calm majesty: "Woman, here is your son ... Here is your mother" (Jn 19:26,27); "I am thirsty" (Jn 19:28); and "It is finished" (Jn 19:30). Read in this way, we discover a development in the Passion narratives from suffering through care for others to serenity.

For us, of course, the stages are not simply chronological. Agony, compassion, and serenity are interwoven in priestly ministry, but our openness and fidelity to these demands – to suffer, to serve, and yet remain serene – create a disposition that can fill our commitment with joy.

Such openness and fidelity do not come easily. I find comfort in Newman's words: "The planting of Christ's cross in the heart is sharp and trying;" – it does not come instinctively for us to plant Christ's cross in our hearts – "but", he goes on, "the stately tree rears itself aloft, and has fair branches and rich fruit, and is good to look upon." (*Parochial and Plain Sermons*). Hold fast. Fidelity bears fruit.

As Jesus' love for us, revealed on the cross, knew no limit, so our response, when offered wholeheartedly, without reserve, will bring joy to our commitment, whatever the cost. And at the end, we will find we can say with him: "It is finished."

Mgr Roderick Strange, Rector of the Pontifical Beda College, Rome.

The Perseverance of the Priest

Dom Antony Sutch OSB

It is strange to draw courage and perseverance from those who have failed even though one could never emulate them. The Apostles Peter and Thomas head a list of lovers of God and ministers of His Son's message, themselves saints, who fell and picked themselves up again and again. They were challenged by the man Jesus, by what he said, did and claimed and by his own personality and by his request to baptise the world. No doubt they struggled to know him and struggled to know how to hold on to faith and hope once he had left them. They must have been puzzled by themselves and by those they met. They must have gone through all the emotions we go through from fear to joy, from doubt to love, from pain and grief to rapture.

Not only does God's Word challenge us in Himself but He challenges us in every person we meet and, of course, in ourselves. Priests are called to be that challenge, to be that contradiction and the sign to all. Their very frailty and humanity is the power of Divine love if they persevere. Ever prepared to be called the whited sepulchre, the hypocrite and the layer of heavy burdens on the backs of others, their perseverance, even if at times faithless, is a witness to a dream, a hope, a consummation, ultimately to the Truth.

Tempted to point the finger, to shun the unpleasant, the outcast, they try to steer the goodly path. They fumble with the complexities of love and its application to a multitude of ethical dilemmas. Shoring up buildings, begging for money, filling in forms, filing policies and ever pursued by bureaucracy they recognise that they are just humans. And as humans they are one with all. Like humans they need others.

Determined to hang on to the coat tails of God they

persist in trying to pray regularly, to talk to God, to learn to know His Son. They draw strength from many before them, whose lives and writings and circumstances simply echo their own and yet they have seemed unbowed by tragedy and evil.

They are especially called by the Church to minister sacraments, to preach the Word: in the words of Isaiah: "The spirit of the Lord is upon me, because he has anointed me to preach good news to the poor. He has sent me to proclaim release to the captives and recovering of sight to the blind, to set at liberty those who are oppressed, to proclaim the acceptable year of the Lord." They realise their flaws, they acknowledge the priesthood of the baptised but their own anointing gives them the resolve to be faithful ministers of the mysteries of God and accept the responsibilities of the priesthood.

Open to God, open to all, they rely utterly on the grace of God and they walk with him and their own people to fullness of life. The glass is dim, the flesh is weak, but the love of God is undaunted. In fact the only question they have to be able to answer, by whomsoever it is asked, even God himself, is: "Do you love me?"

Dom Antony Sutch OSB, Parish Priest of St Benet's, Beccles.

Love Remembered, Love Sustained

Fr Richard Taylor

The priesthood, lived contentedly, is one of the most sustained examples of love among believers. It is love that has transcended the ravages of time. We recall with gratitude those who joined it and join it, and especially those we have loved, not least those who have passed on before us. What would our lives have been without them?

It is traditionally accepted that at the Last Supper Jesus instituted the priesthood. It was the feast of love. The disciples where supposed to be the first in love. That meant that what Jesus had done the disciples should also do – wash the feet of each other, take care of the community, be selfless and self-giving. They were to do these things in memory of Jesus. This was not just to repeat the ritual of the Last Supper. It was to represent everywhere and always the pattern of his life. The Last Supper was a ritual memorial of his whole life and an anticipation of how that life would end in Passion, Death and Resurrection. Jesus had preached the coming of God's kingdom in and through his own person. He was love and forgiveness personified. As St Peter said: "You know the word which he (God) sent to Israel, preaching good news of peace by Jesus Christ (he is Lord of all), the word which was proclaimed through all Judea, beginning from Galilee after the baptism which John preached: how God anointed Jesus of Nazareth with the Holy Spirit and with power; how he went about doing good and healing all that were oppressed by the devil, for God was with him" (Acts 10:36-38).

This is the inspiration of the priesthood. In the Church the priest symbolises by his very existence the values of the kingdom of God. Daily at the altar and in the pulpit, and through personal exchange, he brings to focus the believing aspirations of the faithful. Priests pray to spend their lives with Christ for the faithful with whom they are the Church. John Henry Newman spoke unforgettably about his ministry, which he exercised for over twenty years as an Anglican, and over forty as a Catholic: "O kind and affectionate hearts, O loving friends, should you know anyone whose lot it has been, by writing or by word of mouth, in some degree to help you thus to act; if he has ever told you what you knew about yourselves or what you did not know; has read to you your wants and feelings, and comforted you by the very reading: has made you feel that there was a higher life than this daily one, and a brighter world than that you see; or encouraged you, or sobered you, or opened a way to the enquiring or soothed the perplexed; if what he has said or done has ever made you take interest in him, or feel well inclined towards him; remember such a one in time to come, though you hear him not, and pray for him, that in all things he may know God's will, and at all times he may be ready to fulfil it" (The Parting of Friends, in *Sermons Bearing on Subjects of the Day*).

Any priest will probably feel that his performance never matches his ideals. He can never love enough. That can bring him suffering. But we know that selfless suffering for selfless love is saving. To love and be loved, that is what life is about. And the pressurised priest might never suspect how much he is loved.

> At church, with meek and unaffected grace,
> His looks adorned the venerable place;
> Truth from his lips prevailed with double sway,
> And fools, who came to scoff, remained to pray.
>
> Oliver Goldsmith, 'The Deserted Village'

That is how he is so often seen, for Grace is everywhere (Bernanos), not just in a Longford village long ago, and not just in a splendid novel set in pre-war France.

Fr Richard Taylor is a retired priest of the Diocese of Salford.

A Royal Priesthood

Dom Henry Wansbrough OSB

In its great document on the Church, *Lumen Gentium*, Vatican II insists not only on the sacredness of the ministerial priesthood, but also on the priesthood of the whole People of God: "The faithful, by virtue of their royal priesthood, join in the offering of the Eucharist, and they exercise their priesthood in receiving the sacraments, in prayer and thanksgiving, through the witness of a holy life, by self-denial and by active charity" (*LG*,10).

The ministerial priesthood is a special function in the priesthood exercised by the Body of Christ, the Church, as a whole. It is the Body of Christ which primarily exercises the priesthood of Christ, both in the Eucharist and in the other priestly activities, some of which have just been mentioned. Just as the Eucharist cannot take place without the presidency of an ordained bishop or priest, so *Lumen Gentium* is at pains to show that the laity too have special functions in the priestly office of the Body of Christ (*LG*, 11-12, and especially *LG*, 34: "Jesus Christ, the supreme and eternal priest, wishes to continue his witness and his service also through the laity"). The Scriptural text most frequently quoted in support of this point of view is 1 Peter 2:9, "You are a chosen race, a royal priesthood, a people to be treasured". The translation of the final word of these three descriptive phrases is abnormal. The NJB has "a people to be his personal possession". The NRSV has "God's own people", with a footnote, "Gk *a people for his possession*". It will be enlightening to look at the roots of this quotation.

"A chosen race, a royal priesthood" is taken from the promise of God in Exodus 19:6 that, if Israel obeys his laws, the LORD will take Israel to be his own special people. The third descriptive phrase of 1 Peter comes in Exodus in the previous verse. It is used always of Israel as the special, treasured possession (e.g. Ps 135:4, "possession" in the Grail translation, "treasured possession" in the new Revised Grail). It suggests a possession specially valued and cherished by the owner. I would suggest that the other two phrases (in Hebrew "a kingdom of priests, a holy people") are exegetic, that is, explaining in what way this possession is to be taken to himself and treasured by the LORD. Although the passage comes in the Book of Exodus, the language of Exodus 19:3-8 is clearly Deuteronomic ("kingdom" would have little sense at the time of the Exodus wanderings), expressing the rich theology of Deuteronomy on the close and affectionate relationship between the LORD and Israel, God's son.

Two other elements merit more than a moment's consideration. The priesthood envisaged in this expression is presumably modelled on that of the Deuteronomic Temple service. The aim of this was to express, not only by sacrifice, but also by prayer and cultic purity, the absolute sovereignty of God. It is most forcefully expressed in the "creed" of Deuteronomy 6:4-5: "The LORD our God is one LORD. You must love the LORD your God with all your heart, with all your soul, with all your strength." Secondly, the people is to be holy, with God's own holiness. Israel must also be bathed in that daunting divine holiness which Isaiah glimpsed in the Temple as the seraphim chanted "Holy, holy, holy", and which left him with a withering sense of his own unworthiness. Furthermore, throughout the moral teaching of the Bible Israel is exhorted, "Be holy as I am holy". Created in the image of God, the Israelite must treat others, and especially the stranger, the poor and the unfortunate, with the generosity which God showed to Israel when they were in Egypt. This, too, is part of the priestly ministry of the People of God.

The phrase "kingdom of priests" is used also in Revelation 1:6 and 5:10. Perhaps enough has been said to show the rich and affectionate biblical background to the notion of the People of God as a kingdom of priests.

Dom Henry Wansbrough OSB, former Master of St Benet's Hall, Oxford and Member of the Pontifical Biblical Commission.

The Priest as Preacher

Fr Allan White OP

A pastor, moving to another parish, received some letters of regret from his parishioners. One had a sting in the tail. "We shall particularly miss your sermons; they were like water to a drowning man." Preaching requires humility. It is an expression of the pastoral office of the priest. We preach the Word but we must also be transparent to that Word and not obscure it. We preach the truth of Jesus Christ. It is not our truth; we are its servants. The word we speak is at its most powerful when it springs from our own life of discipleship. In our world people learn much more by example than by precept. Origen, a great preacher, once wrote:

> It is dangerous to talk about God, even if what you say is true. And in fact, it is not only false ideas that are dangerous; even true ones are, if they are not put forth at the right time.

We must be hearers before we presume to speak. We preach what we can never fully understand: the mystery of God disclosed to us in the loving sacrifice of His Son. Preaching is the fruit of our own wrestling with the Word as we struggle to make it part of our lives so that it may become our life. It is distilled through the prayer, the pastoral experience and the study of the pastor. We cannot come cold and unprepared to our preaching, expecting the people of God to be inflamed by the Word in their own lives. We need to clear space in our busy lives, making time for the Word, so that we may speak it in good time and at the right time.

In the synagogue in Nazareth Jesus presents the paradigm for the good homily (Lk 4:21). He took down the scroll, read it and said, "Today this Scripture is being fulfilled in your hearing." The pastor strives to fulfil the Scripture in the corner of the mission field he serves so that his people will recognise Jesus in the breaking of the bread and in the communion of their discipleship.

In our wrestling with the Word certain things are necessary. We must confront the text of Scripture and try to situate it in terms of what has gone before and what will come after it. We must remember that the two Testaments give a single witness to God's providential plan. Above all we must be keen observers of the flock of God entrusted to us and of the environment in which they live. The experience the pastor derives from watching over and listening to his flock will be part of the material he uses to disclose the presence of Christ in his parish. The better observer and listener he is, the more he will know his people and the more the people will find themselves summoned by his preaching to a deeper friendship with the Lord. There is a two-fold study involved in preaching: we look into the Book of Life, which is the Scriptures, and we attempt to read the story of the community we serve. In the end we desire that the people of God see only Jesus. In God's good time that will come about if we love the Word and love those whose pastor we are.

Fr Allan White OP, Socius to the Master of the Dominican Order for the Provinces of North-West Europe and Canada.

Priestly Service and Support

Fr Anthony Wilcox

When I was a teenager and thinking about becoming a priest, the local curate influenced me greatly. He was a genial character, a great role model. I remember two sayings of his that have had a great influence on my life. The first was when I was about fourteen. Another boy and I were helping the curate to set up the Parish Hall for a meeting. The curate said: "If you want to be a priest, then be prepared to move chairs." It was what we were doing at the particular time, but I didn't think it all that "priestly". Saying Mass, visiting the sick, burying the dead, surely these were the "priestly" things.

After ordination I was appointed as a curate, and one of the jobs I had to do was give talks to various parish groups. It always seemed to be me who had to open up the hall and put out the chairs, switch on the kettle and set out the cups. I hated it. Why should the priest have to do all this sort of thing? Surely his job was to lead the people. He should be preparing the talk so that the people coming might benefit from his wisdom.

It was then that I visited my priest friend, by now a venerable parish priest. We talked of what it was like to be a curate, and I mentioned my frustration. He reminded me of what he had said years before and suddenly the penny dropped. He was right. Service of the people includes the menial tasks. Why, the Lord washed his disciples' feet! I still put out the chairs, switch on the tea urn, turn out the lights and lock up, but with a smile. As I do it I say a little prayer for my friend, now gone to the Lord, a thank you prayer for insight into an important part of priesthood.

There was a second saying that my friend gave me. It was after I was ordained: "If another priest comes to your presbytery door, let him in and spend time with him immediately. Especially if he is a stranger. Drop everything. He is very likely in need of priestly support." How true! I have experienced such on a number of occasions. It is all part of brotherly love and brotherly support.

Many of us who have been ordained for more than forty years can remember great gatherings of priests at deanery and diocesan level and of retreats when great numbers of clergy would be present. We recall funerals of priests when it was "de rigueur" to go, whether you knew the priest or not and times when we gathered as curates and complained about our parish priests or our bishops. It was the gathering that mattered. The process of being together helped that bonding and support which is the true hallmark of the Catholic priesthood in this country.

Times have changed rapidly. Two hundred and fifty years ago, our country was mainly rural. It was an era when mutual financial support among the clergy began. Nearly all the sick and retired clergy associations started at this time. No one, neither bishops nor laity, was systematically supporting clergy who were sick or retired. The clergy organised it themselves – and it worked.

The simple fact is that within any group, it is the members themselves who can help each other best, not someone from outside. Married people are the best ones for supporting other married people, teachers for teachers and so on. Dare I say bishops for bishops? I think so. Priests are the best people for helping other priests.

From a rural to an industrial to a post-industrial society – that is what we are now. The pace of change is so rapid. The challenges seem awesome for the priest today. The battering we have had, the tainting of priesthood with child abuse, the fall in Mass attendance, the decline in vocations, the crisis management as bishops try to fill vacant parishes, the additional work as parishes are combined. Then there is the increasing workload, more and more administration, more and more meetings and the newly ordained almost forced to become parish priests before they've learned the ropes.

Where will it end? I don't know. But I know this, that if individual priests are imbued with the idea of service ("moving chairs") and the idea of supporting their brethren, then priesthood and Church will survive.

Fr Anthony Wilcox, Parish Priest of Henley-on-Thames and former Chairman of the National Conference of Priests.

Index of Contributors